GCSE History is always topical with CGP...

Revising AQA's "America, 1920–1973: Opportunity and Inequality" topic is no easy task, but don't worry — this CGP book has the whole half-century covered.

It's packed with crystal-clear revision notes, plenty of helpful activities, sample answers, exam tips and exam-style questions. It's an opportunity not to be missed!

How to access your free Online Edition

This book includes a free Online Edition to read on your PC, Mac or tablet.
To access it, just go to **cgpbooks.co.uk/extras** and enter this code...

0619 4854 0298 1839

By the way, this code only works for one person. If somebody else has used this book before you, they might have already claimed the Online Edition.

CGP — still the best! ☺

Our sole aim here at CGP is to produce the highest quality books —
carefully written, immaculately presented and dangerously close to being funny.

Then we work our socks off to get them out to you
— at the cheapest possible prices.

Published by CGP

Editors:
Andy Cashmore, Robbie Driscoll, Alex Fairer, Catherine Heygate, Harry Millican, Katya Parkes, Jack Tooth

Contributors:
Paddy Gannon

With thanks to Emma Cleasby and Matthew Greenhalgh for the proofreading.

With thanks to Laura Jakubowski, Ana Pungartnik and Emily Smith for the copyright research.

Acknowledgements:

Cover Image: Martin Luther King (1929-1968) American priest activist for Civil Right Movement of black Americans saluting the crowd during the March in Washington on August 28, 1963 / Bridgeman Images.

With thanks to Mary Evans Picture Library for permission to use the images on pages 4, 20, 30, 44 and 48.

Extract on page 5: Stuart Chase, Prosperity: Fact or Myth. Published 1929.

With thanks to Getty Images for permission to use the images on pages 8, 14, 18, 26 and 40.

Extract on page 9: Excerpt from p. 83 from ONLY YESTERDAY: AN INFORMAL HISTORY OF THE NINETEEN-TWENTIES by FREDERICK LEWIS ALLEN. Copyright 1931 by Frederick Lewis Allen, renewed © 1959 by Agnes Rogers Allen. Reprinted by permission of HarperCollins Publishers.

Interpretation 1 on page 16: Extract from Felix Von Luckner, Seeteufel Erobert Amerika. Reprinted in This Was America by Oscar Handlin (1949) © Lilian Handlin, reproduced by permission.

Interpretation 1 on page 21: From ROOSEVELT AND HOPKINS: AN INTIMATE HISTORY by Robert E. Sherwood. Copyright © 1948, 1950 by Robert E. Sherwood. Copyright renewed © 1976, 1978 by Robert E. Sherwood. Used by permission of Brandt & Hochman Literary Agents, Inc. All rights reserved.

Interpretation 2 on page 21: Excerpt from p. 301-302 from ONLY YESTERDAY: AN INFORMAL HISTORY OF THE NINETEEN-TWENTIES by FREDERICK LEWIS ALLEN. Copyright 1931 by Frederick Lewis Allen, renewed © 1959 by Agnes Rogers Allen. Reprinted by permission of HarperCollins Publishers.

Extract on page 31: Excerpt from "The Good War": An Oral History of World War II - Copyright © 1984 by Studs Terkel. Reprinted by permission of The New Press. www.thenewpress.com

Interpretation 1 on page 36: Excerpt from Hard Times: An Oral History of the Great Depression - Copyright © 1970, 1986 by Studs Terkel. Reprinted by permission of The New Press. www.thenewpress.com

Interpretation 2 on page 36: Republished with permission of ABC-CLIO Inc, from This I Remember by Eleanor Roosevelt. Copyright 1949, by Anna Eleanor Roosevelt. Permission conveyed through Copyright Clearance Center, Inc.

Extract on page 39: From THE OTHER AMERICA: POVERTY IN THE UNITED STATES by Michael Harrington. Copyright © 1962, 1969, 1981 by Michael Harrington. Copyright renewed © 1990 by Stephanie Harrington. Reprinted with the permission of Scribner, a division of Simon & Schuster, Inc. All rights reserved.

Extract on page 51: Grofman, Bernard, ed. Legacies of the 1964 Civil Rights Act. pp.9. © 2000 by the Rector and Visitors of the University of Virginia. Reprinted by permission of the University of Virginia Press.

Interpretation 1 on page 53: Reprinted by permission from Political Science Quarterly, 91 (Winter 1976-1977): 601-618.

Interpretation 2 on page 53: From Memoirs of Richard Nixon by Richard Nixon, copyright © 1979. Reprinted by permission of Grand Central Publishing, an imprint of Hachette Book Group, Inc.

With thanks to Rex Features for permission to use the image on page 54.

With thanks to The University Press of Kentucky for permission to use the extract on page 58 from Generation on Fire: Voices of Protest by Jeff Kisseloff. Copyright © 2007 by Jeff Kisseloff. Published by the University Press of Kentucky.

With thanks to Washington University for permission to use the extract on page 58 from an Interview with Stokely Carmichael (Title #967) conducted by Blackside, Inc., for the program Eyes on the Prize II. Henry Hampton Collection, Washington University Libraries. The full interview can be found at http:// digital.wustl.edu/e/eii/eiiweb/car5427.0967.029stokleycarmichael.html

ISBN: 978 1 78908 286 9
Printed by Elanders Ltd, Newcastle upon Tyne.
Clipart from Corel®

Based on the classic CGP style created by Richard Parsons.

Contents

Exam Skills

American People and the 'Boom'

Americans' Experiences of the Depression and New Deal

Post-War America

Exam Hints and Tips

GCSE AQA History is made up of two papers. The papers test different skills and each one covers different topics. These pages give you more information so that you'll know what to expect on the day of the exam.

You will take Two Papers altogether

Paper 1 covers the Period Study and the Wider World Depth Study

Paper 1 is 2 hours long. It's worth 84 marks — 50% of your GCSE. This paper will be divided into two sections:

- Section A: Period Study.
- Section B: Wider World Depth Study.

> This book covers the Period Study America, 1920-1973: Opportunity and Inequality.

> It's really important that you make sure you know which topics you're studying for each paper.

Paper 2 covers the Thematic Study and the British Depth Study

Paper 2 is 2 hours long. It's worth 84 marks — 50% of your GCSE. This paper will be divided into two sections:

- Section A: Thematic Study.
- Section B: British Depth Study. This also includes a question on the Historic Environment.

The Period Study tests Three Different Skills

Interpretation

1) Interpretations express opinions about an event or issue in the past. Questions 1, 2 and 3 in the exam focus on two interpretations which give different views on the same topic.

> Look at Interpretation 1 and Interpretation 2. In what ways do the authors' views differ about segregation? Use both interpretations to explain your answer. [4 marks]

2) For question 1, you'll be asked to identify the main differences between the authors' views.

3) Question 2 will ask you to explain why you think the interpretations give different views. Consider the authors' backgrounds, whether they focused on different areas of the topic, or if they were writing for different purposes.

> Explain why the authors of Interpretation 1 and Interpretation 2 might have different views about segregation. Use both interpretations and your own knowledge in your answer. [4 marks]

4) For question 3, you'll have to explain which interpretation you find more convincing. Decide your opinion before you start writing, and state it clearly at the beginning and end of your answer. You need to explain why you hold that opinion, using evidence from both texts and your own knowledge to support your answer.

> The Interpretation activities in this book will help you to compare interpretations and use them to write a clear, well-structured argument.

> Do you think Interpretation 1 or Interpretation 2 is more convincing about segregation? Use both interpretations and your own knowledge to explain your answer. [8 marks]

Exam Hints and Tips

Knowledge and Understanding

In the exam, you'll need to use your <u>own knowledge</u> and <u>understanding</u> of the topic to back up your answers. This is <u>particularly important</u> in question 4, which will ask you to <u>describe</u> two <u>key features</u> or <u>characteristics</u> of the period.

> Describe two difficulties that African Americans faced during World War Two.   [4 marks]

The <u>Knowledge and Understanding</u> activities in this book will help you to revise <u>key features</u> and <u>events</u> from the period — <u>what</u> was happening, <u>when</u> it was happening, <u>who</u> was involved and all the other <u>important details</u>.

Thinking Historically

1) As well as knowing what happened when, you'll also need to use <u>historical concepts</u> to analyse <u>key events</u> and <u>developments</u>. These include continuity, change, cause and consequence.

> Explain how the lives of Americans were affected by Prohibition.   [8 marks]

2) Question 5 will ask you to explain how something <u>changed</u> as a result of a <u>key event</u> or <u>development</u>. Back up all your points with <u>evidence</u> and <u>explain why</u> the evidence supports the point.

> Which had the more important impact on America in the 1930s, the First New Deal or the Second New Deal? [12 marks]

3) Question 6 will ask you to make a <u>judgement</u> about the <u>importance</u> of two <u>different factors</u>. You need to decide which factor you think is <u>more important</u>, then explain your decision using <u>evidence</u> to support your argument.

The <u>Thinking Historically</u> activities in this book will help you to practise using historical concepts to analyse different parts of the topic.

Remember these Tips for Approaching the Questions

Organise your Time in the exam

1) You'll have to answer <u>six questions</u> for the Period Study part of the exam — it's important to <u>stay organised</u> so that you have time to answer all of the questions.

2) The <u>more marks</u> a question is worth, the <u>longer</u> your answer should be.

3) Don't get carried away writing lots for a question that's only worth 4 marks — you'll need to <u>leave time</u> for the <u>higher mark questions</u>.

> Try to leave a few minutes at the <u>end</u> of the exam to go back and <u>read over</u> your answers.

Stay Focused on the question

1) Read the question <u>carefully</u> — underline the <u>key words</u> so you know exactly what you need to do.

2) Make sure that you <u>answer the question</u>. Don't just chuck in everything you know about the topic.

3) Your answers have got to be <u>relevant</u> and <u>accurate</u> — make sure you include <u>precise details</u> like the <u>dates</u> that important events happened and the <u>names</u> of the people involved in them.

Learn this information and make exam stress history...

There are no marks for spelling, punctuation and grammar in the Period Study, but you should still use a clear writing style — it'll make it easier for the examiner to understand your answers.

Exam Skills

The 'Boom' and its Impact

The US economy boomed in the decade after the First World War — it experienced huge growth. Many Americans prospered as a result of this 'boom' as it made them richer and gave them new opportunities.

The 'Boom' meant that America became a Consumer Society

The US economy was strong in the 1920s. This gave many Americans a feeling of economic security which encouraged them to spend and borrow more money. Employment rates were high and wages increased too.

1) This helped to create a consumer society. People had more money to spend on things like hoovers and washing machines, which were luxury goods at the time. These goods and other expensive products like cars were made more affordable by hire-purchase (where things were paid for in instalments).

2) Credit (when you take out a loan or get given an item and agree to pay for it later) was easy to get. This encouraged people to buy expensive goods that made their standard of living better.

Comment and Analysis

Most Americans weren't worried about debt, as they thought the economy would keep growing and banks would always lend. There was a feeling of economic optimism — people who warned that the economy might fall again were just ignored.

3) Advertising also encouraged Americans to spend more. The 1920s saw a rapid increase in advertising, as companies tried to persuade people to buy their goods. Adverts appeared everywhere — from newspapers and magazines to roadside posters. Companies also advertised using new technologies, such as radio and film, which helped them to reach an even wider audience.

Some companies split their wealth into equal parts called shares. The public can buy and sell shares on the stock market. The value of a company's shares can go up or down.

4) The rise of the consumer society made companies prosper, which meant that the value of shares kept increasing. This encouraged people to keep buying shares, which led to a stock market boom.

5) Many people bought shares using credit, waited for their value to go up, then sold them for profit. This is called speculation. Many speculators became very rich.

Lots of Industries Took Off during the 'Boom'

1) Many new industries prospered in the 1920s, such as the electricity, telephone and chemical industries.

2) The motor industry grew quickly too, as Henry Ford began to use mass production in his car factories:

- The Ford factories created an efficient assembly line system that produced cars in large quantities.
- These cars could be made quickly — in 1925, one of Ford's assembly lines was producing a Ford Model T every ten seconds.
- Cars could also be produced more cheaply. Assembly line construction didn't require skilled workers, so costs were lower for factory owners. As a result, cars were cheaper, and millions of ordinary Americans owned a car by the end of the 1920s.
- Mass production helped Henry Ford and his factories to prosper. Ford workers benefited too — their pay was double the average wage.

A Ford assembly line in 1929.

3) The car industry boosted the steel, glass, rubber and petrol industries. The construction industry also profited from the demand for good roads — petrol stations, motels and roadside restaurants were built across the USA. Car owners were able to live further away from their workplace, so lots of houses were built outside cities in the suburbs.

4) Other industries copied Ford's mass production methods, meaning that items such as radios and fridges were made in huge quantities too. This made these goods cheaper, and more people could afford them.

The 'Boom' and its Impact

The activities on this page will help you get to grips with how the 'boom' affected America during the 1920s.

Thinking Historically

1) Copy and complete the table below, explaining how each factor affected people's lives in America in the 1920s. Give as much detail as possible.

Factor	How it affected people's lives
a) Hire-Purchase	
b) Credit	
c) Advertising	
d) Mass Production	
e) Stock Market Boom	

Interpretation

The interpretation below is from a book by Stuart Chase, published in 1929. Chase was an economics expert in the 1920s. He is explaining the importance of the motor car in America's economic 'boom'.

1) Read the interpretation, then give evidence from page 4 to support each highlighted phrase.

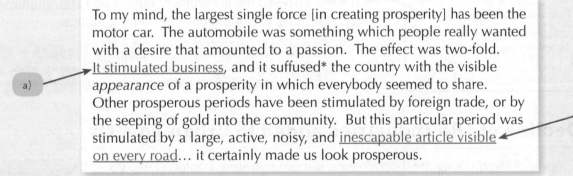

To my mind, the largest single force [in creating prosperity] has been the motor car. The automobile was something which people really wanted with a desire that amounted to a passion. The effect was two-fold. It stimulated business, and it suffused* the country with the visible *appearance* of a prosperity in which everybody seemed to share. Other prosperous periods have been stimulated by foreign trade, or by the seeping of gold into the community. But this particular period was stimulated by a large, active, noisy, and inescapable article visible on every road... it certainly made us look prosperous.

*filled

2) Write a brief summary of Chase's argument. What does he suggest was good about the motor car? Does he think it was as good for everyone in America as it seemed?

BOOM! Now I have your attention...

Make sure you use specific examples in the exam. For example, don't just say that some people benefited from the 'boom' — back this up by mentioning hire-purchase and credit.

The 'Boom' and its Impact

Republican Party policies encouraged the economy to grow, but not all Americans benefited from the 'boom'. The lives of some people got significantly worse, and the government did little to help them.

Some Republican Party Policies added to Prosperity...

1) Republican governments in the 1920s adopted a laissez-faire approach to the economy. This meant that they believed the government shouldn't try to control the economy, so there was little regulation of businesses, banks or the stock market. The government wanted to give businesses the opportunity to be successful, so they placed as few restrictions on them as possible. This attitude played a big role in the 'boom'.

> Republican governments also adopted the idea of 'rugged individualism'. This meant that people were expected to work hard to support themselves, rather than relying on the government for help.

2) The Republican government reduced income tax and made sure that other taxes were low. This meant that people had more money, which they could then spend on the products of US businesses. The government also encouraged banks to lend money and give people credit.

3) In 1922, the government introduced the Fordney-McCumber Tariff. It was meant to protect US farmers and factories by making it costly for foreign producers to import their goods into America. As a result, American goods were always cheaper than foreign goods, since foreign producers had to raise their prices to cover the cost of the tariff. This meant that people were more likely to buy US products.

... but there was Poverty in Rural Areas

1) Demand for food was high in Europe during the First World War, so many US farms expanded and sold goods to foreign countries. European farms recovered after the war, but US farmers carried on producing too much — this overproduction caused prices to plunge. Many farms ran at a loss.

2) Some farmers had taken out bank loans to expand their farms during the war. When they failed to pay these back, their debts increased. Many had to sell their farms and travel around the country to find work.

3) The textile industry started using man-made synthetic fibres, so the demand for cotton decreased. Cotton was a key crop in the South, so this decline hit many southern farmers and added to rural poverty.

Comment and Analysis

Coolidge vetoed the bill as it showed that prosperity wasn't benefiting everyone. Some said the Republicans were happy to ignore poverty to make it look like they'd created a country where everyone could prosper.

4) The McNary-Haugen Bill was proposed many times in the 1920s to help struggling farmers, but President Coolidge vetoed it twice. The bill involved the government buying up extra supplies of key farm products to stop farmers from losing money.

> Many African Americans in southern states were sharecroppers — farmers who rented land in exchange for some of their crops. They lived in extreme poverty and suffered discrimination due to segregation (see p.44).

The Decline of Old Industries added to Urban Poverty

Newer industries thrived during the 'boom' years, but old industries couldn't keep up.

1) The coal industry struggled to compete with the oil industry. New mining technologies led to coal workers being sacked, and miners who kept their jobs were paid less.

> Urban poverty was a big problem in those towns that relied on old industries.

2) Monopolies (where a whole industry, such as steel or oil, is owned or controlled by one company or group) kept prices high and wages low, as there was no competition from other companies for customers or workers.

3) Millions of farmers migrated from rural areas to towns to find work. This increased urban poverty, as more people had to compete for the same jobs and housing.

Comment and Analysis

Lots of people didn't prosper in the 1920s. There was a big gap in wealth between the rich and poor. The poorest 60% of the people owned less than 5% of the wealth. Certain social groups didn't prosper — for example, working-class women were very poorly paid.

> Many African Americans migrated to northern towns to find factory work. Prejudice and poverty often forced them to live in poor areas.

American People and the 'Boom'

The 'Boom' and its Impact

The 'boom' of the 1920s brought prosperity to some Americans, but a lot of people were still stuck in poverty. This page will help you get your head around some of the more negative sides of the 'boom'.

Knowledge and Understanding

1) The Republican Party adopted a laissez-faire approach to the US economy in the 1920s. What does this mean?

2) What is meant by the term 'rugged individualism'?

3) Copy and complete the mind map below by adding problems faced by American farmers during the 1920s. Give as much detail as possible.

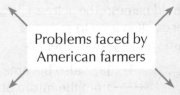

Problems faced by American farmers

Thinking Historically

1) Explain how each of the ideas or policies below contributed to America's prosperity in the 1920s.

a) Laissez-Faire   b) Tax Reductions   c) Fordney-McCumber Tariff

2) Copy and complete the diagram below, explaining how people's lives were affected by each factor in the 1920s.

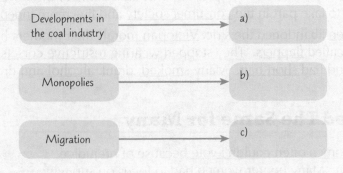

Developments in the coal industry → a)

Monopolies → b)

Migration → c)

The 'boom' didn't benefit everyone...

If you're asked about how life changed for Americans during the 1920s, remember to consider the experiences of different groups of people. Many people didn't prosper during the 'boom'.

American People and the 'Boom'

Social and Cultural Developments

The 1920s saw significant social and cultural <u>change</u> in America. The <u>entertainment industry</u> became an important part of <u>everyday life</u> across the country, and <u>women</u> gained new <u>opportunities</u> and <u>freedoms</u>.

The Entertainment Industry became very Influential

1) <u>Cinema</u> was a very popular form of entertainment in 1920s America. It used impressive, <u>cutting-edge technology</u>, and although movie theatres were often <u>grand</u> and <u>extravagant</u> places, tickets were <u>cheap</u>. Cinemas opened in <u>every town</u>, and by 1926, around <u>100 million</u> Americans went to watch a film <u>every week</u>.

2) In the early 1920s, all films were <u>silent</u>. This changed in 1927 with the release of '<u>The Jazz Singer</u>' — it was the first feature film to include <u>audio</u>. These films became known as '<u>talkies</u>' and attracted yet more people to the cinema.

3) The rise of the cinema saw <u>movie stars</u> such as <u>Gloria Swanson</u> and <u>Rudolph Valentino</u> become household names. The actress <u>Clara Bow</u> also became very popular. Audiences often tried to copy her <u>style</u> and <u>behaviour</u>, and she became an <u>icon</u> of the decade.

© John Kobal Foundation / Contributor / Moviepix / Getty Images

Jazz was often performed in <u>speakeasies</u> (see p.14), where young people also <u>drank</u> alcohol and <u>smoked</u>. Its <u>fast-paced</u> rhythm led to <u>daring</u> and <u>suggestive</u> dancing. Many <u>older people</u> thought this behaviour was <u>immoral</u>, so <u>disapproved</u> of jazz.

4) <u>Jazz</u> also became very popular in the 1920s. It developed from the music of <u>black communities</u> in the southern states. Although racism was a huge problem in America at this time (see p.10), many black artists, such as <u>Louis Armstrong</u>, achieved <u>mainstream success</u> through the popularity of jazz.

The Position Of Women in Society began to Change...

1) During the <u>First World War</u>, large numbers of <u>women</u> entered the <u>workforce</u> to fill in for the men who had gone to fight. Women took on jobs usually reserved for men, such as <u>construction work</u>, and also played a <u>key role</u> in the <u>war effort</u> by working in <u>munitions factories</u> and <u>agriculture</u>.

Before WWI, women who worked had traditionally '<u>female</u>' jobs, such as <u>servants</u> and <u>nurses</u>.

2) The <u>huge contribution</u> they made during the war helped groups who had been fighting to secure the <u>vote</u> for women. It became harder to deny women the right to <u>political equality</u> — in <u>1920</u>, the <u>19th Amendment</u> was approved, which gave American women the right to <u>vote</u>.

3) In the 1920s, the number of women in the workforce continued to <u>rise</u>. By 1930, around a <u>quarter of women</u> in America were employed. This gave some of these women the <u>money</u> and <u>freedom</u> to take part in the <u>consumer society</u> and live more <u>independently</u>.

4) Many <u>younger women</u> abandoned the strict <u>Victorian morals</u> their mothers had held. These women were called <u>flappers</u>. They stopped wearing <u>restrictive corsets</u>, wore make-up and <u>loose</u> dresses, and had <u>short hair</u>. Many <u>smoked</u>, drank <u>alcohol</u> and drove <u>cars</u>.

...but life Stayed The Same for Many

1) <u>African-American women</u> often <u>couldn't vote</u> because of prejudice and racism (see p.10). Many <u>poorer women</u> had to focus on <u>surviving</u> and not on <u>joining political campaigns</u> to gain more rights.

As well as looking after the home, many poorer women had to take on <u>extra work</u> to help <u>support</u> their families.

Comment and Analysis

Many American women remained <u>poor</u> in the 1920s — they didn't <u>benefit</u> from the economic 'boom'. Most women also <u>continued</u> to live by <u>traditional values</u>.

2) Even though they won the <u>vote</u> and went into the <u>workplace</u> in bigger numbers, women were still <u>expected</u> to <u>raise children</u>, do housework and stick to <u>Victorian morals</u>.

3) Most women <u>didn't</u> embrace the <u>flapper lifestyle</u>. Many <u>couldn't afford</u> the new <u>fashions</u>, and some <u>religious women</u> didn't <u>approve</u> of flapper behaviour.

Social and Cultural Developments

Use this page to boost your knowledge about the changes to American society and culture during the 1920s.

Knowledge and Understanding

1) Why do you think that the cinema was popular in America during the 1920s? Copy and complete the mind map below, giving as many reasons as you can.

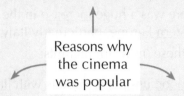

Reasons why the cinema was popular

2) What is jazz? Why did some people disapprove of it in the 1920s?

3) Explain what a 'flapper' was in 1920s America.

4) Give three reasons why most women didn't get involved in the flapper lifestyle.

Interpretation

The interpretation below is from a book by Frederick Lewis Allen, published in 1931. Allen was an American who worked as a journalist in the 1920s, and the book contains his observations on the decade. He is describing a 'revolution' in the way that Americans were expected to behave.

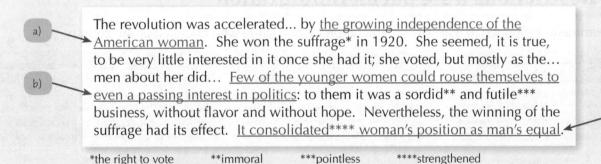

a) The revolution was accelerated... by <u>the growing independence of the American woman</u>. She won the suffrage* in 1920. She seemed, it is true, to be very little interested in it once she had it; she voted, but mostly as the... men about her did... b) <u>Few of the younger women could rouse themselves to even a passing interest in politics</u>: to them it was a sordid** and futile*** business, without flavor and without hope. Nevertheless, the winning of the suffrage had its effect. c) <u>It consolidated**** woman's position as man's equal</u>.

*the right to vote   **immoral   ***pointless   ****strengthened

1) For each highlighted phrase above, explain what it suggests about the lives of women in 1920s America.

2) For each highlighted phrase above, explain whether or not you think it is convincing about the lives of women in 1920s America. Use information from page 8 to explain your answers.

The 19th Amendment — it certainly gets my vote...

When you're giving your opinion on an interpretation, it's really important that you use your own knowledge of the topic to back up your view — always give as much detail as you can.

American People and the 'Boom'

Intolerance and Prejudice

1920s America was a <u>divided society</u>, where immigrants and African Americans suffered from <u>discrimination</u>.

Immigrants suffered Discrimination in their Daily Lives

1) Most <u>immigrants</u> who came to America before 1890 were from <u>northern European</u> countries, like Britain and Germany. Many were <u>well-educated</u>, <u>skilled</u> workers. They <u>thrived</u> in the US and held <u>powerful positions</u> in society by the 1920s. They became known as <u>WASPs</u> — white, Anglo-Saxon Protestants.

2) Between the 1890s and 1920, there was a huge <u>increase</u> in the number of immigrants moving to America from <u>southern</u> and <u>eastern Europe</u>, particularly Italy, Russia and Poland.

3) Many Americans <u>disapproved</u> of these 'new' immigrants:

- 'New' immigrants were often <u>poor</u>, <u>unskilled</u> workers with <u>little education</u>. Some Americans believed they wouldn't be able to <u>contribute</u> to society.

- Others worried that too much <u>cheap immigrant labour</u> would create <u>competition</u> for jobs and cause wages to <u>fall</u>.

- There were fears that some immigrants were <u>communists</u> who wanted to <u>undermine</u> the American way of life. This <u>xenophobia</u> (fear of foreigners) increased when the <u>Red Scare</u> got worse in 1919 (see p.12).

- The majority of Americans were <u>Protestant</u>, but 'new' immigrants were mainly <u>Catholics</u> and <u>Jews</u>. They therefore held different <u>cultural</u> and <u>religious</u> beliefs to most of the US population.

- Immigrants were blamed for <u>social issues</u>, such as <u>crime</u>, <u>alcoholism</u> and the spread of <u>diseases</u>.

> Many 'new' immigrants settled together in <u>separate communities</u>, spoke their <u>own languages</u> and had their <u>own way of life</u>. This lack of <u>integration</u> into US society caused <u>tension</u>.

4) This meant that immigrants were treated with <u>distrust</u> and <u>suspicion</u>. People felt threatened and feared that immigration would completely <u>change</u> America's <u>society</u> and <u>identity</u>.

5) Employers <u>exploited</u> immigrants, expecting them to work <u>long hours</u> for <u>little pay</u>. As a result, immigrants could only afford housing in the <u>poorest</u> parts of the city, where conditions were often <u>cramped</u> and <u>dirty</u>.

New Restrictions were put on Immigration

The government <u>responded</u> to fears over immigration by <u>restricting</u> who could enter the country.

From <u>1917</u>, immigrants were required to pass a <u>literacy test</u> in order to enter the USA. This favoured <u>educated</u> immigrants, who mostly came from wealthier, <u>western European</u> countries. However, immigration policies became even <u>stricter</u> in the <u>1920s</u>.	In <u>1921</u>, the <u>Emergency Quota Act</u> was passed — it introduced a <u>quota system</u> that limited how many people from <u>certain countries</u> were allowed to enter the USA. It particularly <u>restricted</u> immigration from <u>southern</u> and <u>eastern Europe</u>.	In <u>1924</u>, the <u>Johnson-Reed Act</u> put <u>even more limits</u> on immigration, which made it <u>harder</u> for Africans, Asians, Arabs, and eastern and southern Europeans to get into the USA. This act was passed partly because of <u>fear of foreigners</u> and <u>racism</u>. It was supposed to <u>exclude</u> certain races from the USA.

African Americans faced Discrimination throughout the USA

1) <u>Segregation</u> (see p.44) oppressed African Americans in the <u>South</u>, <u>forcing</u> them to use <u>separate</u> facilities to <u>white people</u>. Discrimination in <u>jobs</u> and <u>housing</u> meant that African Americans often lived in <u>poverty</u>.

2) Between 1916 and 1929, large numbers of African Americans in the South <u>moved</u> to the <u>North</u> to find <u>work</u>. Segregation <u>wasn't enforced</u> by law in the North, but <u>racism</u> and <u>prejudice</u> were widespread.

3) This made life <u>hard</u> for African Americans. There were <u>few</u> employment opportunities — many firms <u>refused to hire</u> African Americans, and any work they could find was often <u>unskilled</u> and <u>badly paid</u>.

4) Discrimination forced African Americans to live in <u>ghettos</u> in <u>poor</u> areas of the city. These ghettos could often be <u>run-down</u> and <u>overcrowded</u>. Despite this, African Americans were often charged <u>high rents</u>.

Intolerance and Prejudice

SKILLS PRACTICE

Try these activities to help you to understand American attitudes towards race and immigration in the 1920s.

Knowledge and Understanding

1) Where did the majority of immigrants to America come from before 1890?

2) How did the nature of immigration to America change from 1890 onwards?

3) Copy and complete the mind map below by explaining how each factor created opposition to 'new' immigration.

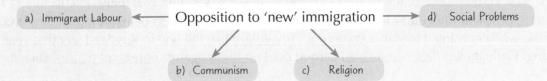

a) Immigrant Labour ← Opposition to 'new' immigration → d) Social Problems

b) Communism   c) Religion

4) Using the following key words and phrases, describe what living in America was like for 'new' immigrants.

separate communities   tension   work   housing

5) Copy and complete the table below by giving the year that each government policy was introduced and explaining how it limited immigration to America.

Policy	Year	How it limited immigration
a) Literacy Tests		
b) The Emergency Quota Act		
c) The Johnson-Reed Act		

Thinking Historically

1) How did life change for African Americans who moved from the South to the North between 1916 and 1929? Give as much detail as possible.

2) In what ways did life stay the same for African Americans who moved from the South to the North between 1916 and 1929?

EXAM TIP

Immigrants and African Americans were treated badly...

It's important to understand how society was divided in the 1920s. Make sure you know the different groups in America who faced intolerance and prejudice and how they were treated.

American People and the 'Boom'

Intolerance and Prejudice

Action was taken against immigrants and African Americans out of fear that they posed a threat to US society.

The Red Scare was at its height between 1919 and 1920

From 1917, Americans worried their way of life was at risk of being destroyed by those who disagreed with capitalism. This period of fear is called the Red Scare, and it was prompted by the rise of two political ideas.

> In 1917, there was a communist revolution in Russia. Communists want wealth to be shared more equally. They often believe that government control over the economy can help to achieve this.

> Anarchists believe that laws and government are unnecessary. The anarchist movement in the USA wanted to get rid of the government.

1) America is a capitalist country. This means that anyone is free to make a profit from their work, and that wealth isn't shared equally. Many Americans worried foreign communists and anarchists might come to the USA and try to change their society. These fears got worse after two major events in 1919.

2) In 1919, post-war difficulties led workers in Seattle to go on strike to demand fair wages. Many worried that the workers wanted to start a communist revolution like the one in Russia. Later that year, supporters of Luigi Galleani (an Italian anarchist) carried out bombings against important figures, such as politicians.

The Red Scare led to greater Intolerance of Immigrants

1) After the bombings in 1919, the government arrested suspected communists and anarchists in a series of operations called the Palmer Raids. Those arrested in the Palmer Raids were mostly immigrants, as they were often held responsible for bringing radical views to America. Hundreds of them were deported, even if they'd done nothing wrong.

> Some said the Palmer Raids were against the Constitution (see p.24). Many of the arrests were made without warrants (permission from legal authorities), so were illegal.

2) In 1921, two Italian anarchists called Nicola Sacco and Bartolomeo Vanzetti were convicted of murder and robbery. Many thought the justice system discriminated against them because of their political views and their status as Italian immigrants.

Sacco & Vanzetti Case
- When Sacco and Vanzetti were arrested, police found anti-government leaflets in their car. It was also revealed that they had gone to Mexico during the First World War to avoid being called up to serve in the US Army. This made the two men seem unpatriotic.
- It is thought that the judge in their trial was biased against Sacco and Vanzetti. He disregarded 107 witness statements that said the two men had been seen elsewhere at the time of the crime.
- There was no clear-cut evidence that Sacco and Vanzetti were guilty, and another criminal even confessed, but the judge refused to give them a second trial. They were executed in 1927.

The Ku Klux Klan targeted African Americans and Immigrants

1) The Ku Klux Klan (KKK) was a white supremacist organisation based in the southern states. They wanted to keep America white and Protestant — the main targets of their hostility were African Americans, but they were also prejudiced against 'new' immigrants, who were often Catholics and Jews.

2) The KKK were first active in the 1860s, but gained new popularity in the North in the 1920s, as levels of 'new' immigration rose and African Americans moved to cities. The KKK appealed to WASPs (see p.10) who felt threatened by these changes in society, and by 1925, KKK membership had grown to around 4 million.

> These crimes often went unpunished, as the justice system was controlled by WASPs or even KKK members.

3) Klan members committed violent crimes to intimidate and kill minorities. Their targets were often kidnapped, tarred and feathered (where hot tar and feathers were applied to the skin) or lynched (hung by a mob).

4) In 1925, Indiana KKK leader D.C. Stephenson was convicted of raping and murdering a white woman. The organisation lost support and political power after this scandal.

Intolerance and Prejudice

Many Americans discriminated against 'new' immigrants and African Americans, as did the US government. These activities will help you to understand how minorities were affected.

Knowledge and Understanding

1) In your own words, describe what each of the following groups believe.

a) Communists   b) Anarchists

2) America is a capitalist country. What does this mean?

3) The flowchart below shows the development of the Red Scare. Copy and complete the flowchart by adding as much information as you can underneath each heading.

a) Fear of anarchism and communism in America → b) Strike in Seattle → c) Bombings → d) Palmer Raids

4) How did prejudice affect the outcome of the Sacco and Vanzetti case? Give as much detail as possible.

5) What was the Ku Klux Klan? Which groups of people did it target?

6) Complete the mind map below by giving reasons for the rise and fall in popularity of the Ku Klux Klan during the 1920s.

a) Rise in Popularity ← Ku Klux Klan → b) Fall in Popularity

Thinking Historically

1) Copy and complete the mind map below by describing the difficulties faced by each group of people as a result of intolerance and prejudice in 1920s America. Use information from pages 10 and 12 to help you.

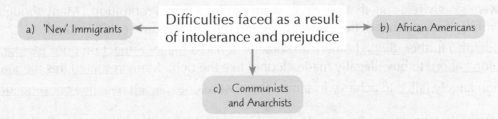

a) 'New' Immigrants ← Difficulties faced as a result of intolerance and prejudice → b) African Americans
↓
c) Communists and Anarchists

Intolerance and Prejudice — Austen's least popular novel...

For the final question in the exam, you'll be asked to focus on two bullet points. Make sure that you write about both bullet points in your answer, or you won't be able to get full marks.

Prohibition and Organised Crime

From 1920 to 1933, it was illegal to make, distribute or sell alcohol in the USA. This was the Prohibition era. When Prohibition was introduced, it both revealed and increased divides in American society.

Prohibition was meant to Improve Morality

1) Temperance movements had been trying to get people to stop drinking alcohol since the 19th century. They said that alcohol caused violence, immoral behaviour and the breakdown of family life.

2) In 1913, temperance groups started to campaign for Prohibition to become law throughout the USA. This gained support from people who thought that Prohibition might improve society.

3) Support for Prohibition reflected the divide between rural and urban America. Many rural Americans were concerned about how US society was changing — they associated alcohol with high crime rates and violence in the rapidly growing cities.

> The middle class blamed alcohol for immorality among 'new' immigrants (see p.10) and the working class. Employers said it made workers unreliable. Many women's groups thought Prohibition would reduce domestic violence.

> In 1919, the 18th Amendment was approved — it banned the production, distribution and sale of alcohol in the USA. This was called Prohibition — it started in 1920.

Prohibition led to a rise in Organised Crime

1) Enforcing Prohibition was impossible, as the public still wanted to buy alcohol.

2) This demand led to people distributing alcohol illegally. People known as moonshiners made their own liquor, and rum-runners smuggled alcohol into the USA. Bootleggers took alcohol that was meant to be used in industry and made it drinkable. Illegal drinking clubs called speakeasies also sprang up.

3) Gangs in cities all over America fought for control over the illegal distribution of alcohol:

© Bettmann / Contributor / Bettmann / Getty Images

- One of the most powerful gang leaders in 1920s America was Al Capone. He fought other gangsters in Chicago to run the city's speakeasies.

- This battle for control led to extreme violence and hundreds of murders. Members of rival gangs were targeted and killed by Capone and his men.

- Capone was very successful — he was influential in US society and earned huge amounts of money. The police never managed to convict Capone for his violent crimes and alcohol distribution — he was only sent to prison for tax evasion.

Opposition to Prohibition Increased in 1929

1) There was always strong opposition to Prohibition in urban areas, especially in the North. Opposition increased during the Depression (see p.18) — people thought Prohibition was bad for the economy. For example, alcohol taxes and jobs in alcohol production could have boosted the economy.

2) People were slowly realising that criminals were profiting from Prohibition. Many thought that, if Prohibition was ended, the government and the public could profit instead.

3) Prohibition also further divided American society. It had a bigger impact on poor people, as they couldn't afford to buy illegally made alcohol like the rich. Many resented this inequality.

4) Prohibition largely failed to achieve its aims. There were unexpected negative consequences instead:

- Although drinking did go down under Prohibition, it didn't make people stop drinking altogether.

- While fewer crimes linked to alcohol and drunkenness were committed, organised crime became more of an issue.

> Roosevelt promised to repeal Prohibition in his 1932 presidential campaign. The 18th Amendment was finally withdrawn in December 1933.

- The rise in organised crime made society more corrupt. Gangsters bribed judges and policemen to overlook their illegal behaviour.

- Prohibition had a negative impact on public health. Poor quality alcohol caused many deaths.

Prohibition and Organised Crime

Prohibition was meant to tackle a range of problems — this page will help you to see how and why it failed.

Knowledge and Understanding

1) Copy and complete the timeline below, adding the key events in the development of Prohibition. Give as much detail as possible.

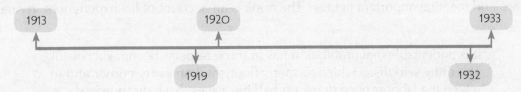

| 1913 | | 1920 | | 1933 |

| 1919 | | 1932 |

2) Give three examples of groups who supported the introduction of Prohibition in America. For each group, explain why they wanted Prohibition to be introduced.

3) Write a short definition for each of the following key terms:

a) Moonshiners b) Rum-Runners c) Bootleggers d) Speakeasies

4) How did Al Capone benefit from Prohibition? Give as much detail as possible.

Thinking Historically

1) Copy and complete the mind map below by explaining the consequences of Prohibition for America. Give as much detail as possible under each heading.

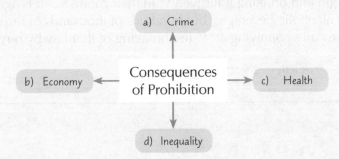

a) Crime

b) Economy ← Consequences of Prohibition → c) Health

d) Inequality

2) Overall, do you think that the consequences of Prohibition were positive or negative for America? Explain your answer.

Prohibition? It seemed like a good idea at the time...

It's important to keep your exam answers focused on the question given to you — at the end of each paragraph, it's helpful to spell out exactly how the point you've made answers the question.

Exam-Style Questions

The exam-style questions on these pages will help you to practise writing about America during the 'boom'.

Interpretation 1

The interpretation below is from a book by Felix von Luckner, published in 1928. Von Luckner was a German nobleman who went on a high-profile visit to America in the late 1920s, making speeches and meeting important figures. The book is an account of his experiences in America.

> It is undeniable that prohibition has in some respects been... successful. The filthy saloons... which formerly flourished on every corner and in which the laborer once drank off half his wages, have disappeared. Now he can instead buy his own car, and ride off for a weekend or a few days with his wife and children in the country or at the sea... The number of crimes and misdemeanors* that originated in drunkenness has declined.

*minor offences

Interpretation 2

The interpretation below is from a magazine article by Pauline Sabin, published in 1928. Sabin was a Republican Party official who had cautiously opposed Prohibition from the mid-1920s. She later became a lot more outspoken and resigned from the party in 1929.

> It is true that we no longer see the corner saloon; but in many cases has it not... moved to the back of a store or up one flight [of stairs] under the name of a "speak-easy"? It is true that... groups of boys can no longer go... and drink their beer genially* and in the open. Is it not true that they are making their own gin and drinking it furtively** in their rooms?... It is against the law to sell alcoholic beverages, but hundreds of thousands of respected citizens are daily conniving at*** the breaking of that law by buying it.

*sociably   **secretly   ***taking part in

Exam-Style Questions

Exam-Style Questions

1) Look at Interpretation 1 and Interpretation 2. In what ways do the authors' views differ about the impact of Prohibition? Use both interpretations to explain your answer.   [4 marks]

2) Explain why the authors of Interpretation 1 and Interpretation 2 might have different views about the impact of Prohibition. Use both interpretations and your own knowledge in your answer.   [4 marks]

3) Do you think Interpretation 1 or Interpretation 2 is more convincing about the impact of Prohibition? Use both interpretations and your own knowledge to explain your answer.   [8 marks]

4) Describe two difficulties that 'new' immigrants to America faced in the 1920s.   [4 marks]

5) Explain how the lives of Americans were affected by the 'boom' of the 1920s.   [8 marks]

6) Look at the bullet points below. Which one was the more important reason for inequalities in America in the 1920s?

   • social reasons
   • economic reasons

   Explain your answer, referring to both bullet points.   [12 marks]

America in the Depression

In <u>1929</u>, the Wall Street stock market <u>crashed</u>, leading to a serious, decade-long <u>depression</u>.

The Economic Effects of the Wall Street Crash were Immediate

Constant <u>buying</u> and <u>selling</u> on the stock market <u>inflated</u> share prices, which made shares <u>seem</u> more <u>valuable</u> than they really were. In <u>1929</u>, the market <u>collapsed</u> — people realised that many businesses were doing <u>badly</u>, so they <u>panicked</u> and tried to <u>sell</u> their shares. After this, it was almost impossible to get <u>credit</u> and the stock market <u>declined</u>. Since the US economy <u>relied</u> on credit, the crash led to an <u>economic depression</u>.

1) From <u>1929</u> to <u>1931</u>, <u>industrial production</u> dropped by a third — <u>wages fell</u> and workers were <u>sacked</u>.

2) Many Americans <u>couldn't afford</u> to pay back bank <u>loans</u> and <u>stopped depositing money</u> in the bank. This forced many banks to <u>close</u>, which meant that people's <u>savings were lost</u>.

3) Banks would no longer give <u>credit</u> to customers, so many people didn't have the money to buy <u>consumer goods</u> anymore. This <u>lack of demand</u> caused businesses to <u>close</u>, so people <u>lost</u> their <u>jobs</u>.

The Social Effects of the Depression were Very Serious

1) Around <u>5.5%</u> of workers were <u>unemployed</u> in <u>1929</u>. By <u>1933</u>, <u>25%</u> of the American workforce was unemployed. Many were out of work for <u>years</u>.

2) This led to <u>severe poverty</u> and <u>starvation</u>. America didn't have a national welfare system or <u>unemployment benefits</u> — people were expected to <u>look after themselves</u>.

3) Many relied on <u>relief schemes</u> set up by <u>local governments</u> and <u>charities</u> which provided food, clothing and accommodation. People queueing for food in '<u>bread lines</u>' became a common sight on American <u>streets</u>.

People at a soup kitchen set up by Al Capone in Chicago, 1930.

4) <u>Hundreds of thousands</u> of people became <u>homeless</u> — <u>relief schemes</u> were able to provide shelter for some, but many ended up sleeping on the <u>streets</u>.

5) <u>Family life</u> was affected — <u>marriages</u> were <u>delayed</u> and the <u>birth rate fell</u>. Many families had to leave their homes to <u>seek work</u>, while some fathers <u>abandoned</u> their families in search of work.

The Depression made things Worse for Farmers...

1) Farmers were already struggling due to <u>overproduction</u> (see p.6), but the crash made <u>prices</u> so <u>low</u> that it <u>wasn't worth</u> taking crops and produce to market. Farmers' <u>debts increased</u> — many couldn't pay their <u>mortgages</u> and were <u>evicted</u> or became <u>tenant farmers</u> (they farmed land owned by someone else).

2) A long series of <u>droughts</u> in the Midwest made things <u>worse</u> — huge areas of land became a '<u>Dust Bowl</u>', which meant that <u>no crops</u> could be grown there.

3) <u>Farm workers</u> roamed around the country seeking <u>work</u>. Many moved to <u>California</u> in search of <u>land</u> to farm, or <u>jobs</u>, but work was <u>scarce</u> and employers <u>exploited</u> migrant farmers.

... and Businessmen Suffered too

1) As the economy collapsed, thousands of <u>businesses</u> went <u>bankrupt</u>. Many businessmen lost their <u>livelihoods</u> and became <u>unemployed</u>.

The Depression <u>didn't</u> make <u>all</u> businessmen <u>suffer</u> — the <u>very wealthy</u> and those who had invested in things like <u>property</u> weren't affected as much.

2) <u>Banks</u> would no longer give out <u>loans</u> after the crash which meant that businesses couldn't <u>find</u> the money they needed to <u>survive</u>. Struggling banks also demanded that businesses <u>repay</u> their existing loans — this <u>forced</u> many businesses to <u>close</u>.

3) <u>Before</u> the crash took place, many American businesses had been suffering from <u>overproduction</u>. <u>Mass production</u> had caused the <u>supply</u> of many goods to be <u>greater</u> than the public <u>demand</u> for them — <u>businessmen</u> were paying to <u>produce</u> goods that <u>weren't being sold</u>, so they weren't making any <u>profit</u>. The crash made this problem <u>even worse</u>, as people had <u>less money</u> to spend on goods.

America in the Depression

America's economic 'boom' came to a disastrous end when the stock market crashed in 1929. These activities will help you to understand how this affected people's lives and the economy.

Knowledge and Understanding

1) The flowchart below shows the development of the Wall Street Crash in 1929. Copy and complete the flowchart, adding as much information as you can underneath each heading.

a) The value of shares → b) The stock market collapse → c) The availability of credit

2) Describe the impact of the stock market crash on each of the following areas of the US economy from 1929 to 1933.

   a) Production
   b) Banks
   c) Businesses

3) Why were farmers unable to pay their mortgages in the Depression? What happened to these farmers?

4) What was the 'Dust Bowl'? How did it make the Depression worse for farmers?

5) Explain why overproduction was a particularly serious problem for businesses during the Depression. Give as much detail as possible.

6) Why did some businessmen not suffer as much as others during the Depression?

Thinking Historically

1) Copy and complete the mind map below by explaining the social consequences of the Depression for Americans. Give as much detail as possible under each heading.

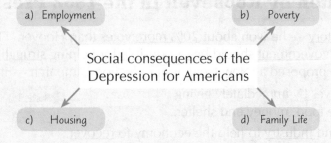

a) Employment   b) Poverty

Social consequences of the Depression for Americans

c) Housing   d) Family Life

I used to buy and sell shares, but I never got credit for it...

The Depression didn't just have an impact on the economy — it changed people's lives too. Make sure you know about the full range of consequences of events such as the Depression.

Americans' Experiences of the Depression and New Deal

Hoover and Roosevelt

President Herbert Hoover, a Republican, was in power at the time of the Wall Street Crash, but in 1932 a presidential election took place. A Democrat called Franklin Delano Roosevelt (FDR) was elected.

Hoover's policies Didn't Do Enough to Support the Population

1) Immediately after the crash, President Hoover did very little to intervene. He believed in rugged individualism (see p.6), so didn't offer direct relief, like food, money and shelter, to individuals. He thought that if he created the right conditions, then people could work themselves out of poverty.

2) He made sure that the government didn't spend more than it received in taxes, but refused to become more involved in economic recovery.

A 'Hooverville' in New York, 1932.

© Mary Evans / Everett Collection

3) As the Depression continued, however, Hoover and his Republican government began to introduce policies to tackle its impact more directly. However, these policies were mostly ineffective — they didn't give people the help they urgently needed:

The Smoot-Hawley Tariff was created in 1930. It raised the price of imported goods to encourage people to buy goods made in the US. →	The tariff harmed recovery. Other countries responded by raising the price of imported US goods, and trade to and from the US fell.
The National Credit Corporation opened in 1931. All major banks were meant to pay into a loan fund to stop struggling banks from closing. →	The scheme failed, as most banks didn't want to help their rivals and believed the government should create the fund instead.
The Reconstruction Finance Corporation (RFC), which formed in 1932, gave out loans to stop businesses and banks from failing. →	It was hoped that the RFC would benefit everyone, but it didn't give individuals the direct relief they needed, so had very little impact.
The Federal Home Loan Bank Act was introduced in 1932 to encourage banks to offer more mortgages and to make home ownership cheaper. →	Despite this, many people were still losing their homes. Some homeless people built shanty towns that were nicknamed 'Hoovervilles'.

People Lost Confidence in Hoover

1) Between 1929 and 1932, banks and businesses continued to fail, and poverty, unemployment and homelessness levels rose sharply across America. Hoover's inadequate response to this caused him to lose support in Congress — this made people a lot less confident in his ability to lead.

2) Hoover's failure to end the Depression made him unpopular with the public. Many saw his refusal to directly support people in need as heartless. His name was linked to the negative effects of the Depression (e.g. 'Hoovervilles').

3) In July 1932, Hoover used force to make the Bonus Army marchers leave Washington DC. A few marchers were killed. This incident made Hoover even more unpopular.

> Congress is the part of the US government which is responsible for making laws.

> The Bonus Army were World War I veterans who were owed compensation payments, but not until 1945. They marched on Washington to demand the right to get the payments early, but the government said no.

Hoover was Beaten by Roosevelt in the 1932 Presidential Election

Roosevelt won a huge victory — he won about 20% more votes than Hoover. FDR offered something different. He thought the government should be responsible for helping struggling US citizens caught up in the Depression. He proposed a 'New Deal' in his election campaign — it had three main aims:

1) To improve people's lives by immediately giving them direct relief, like food, money and shelter.

> These three aims became known as the 'Three Rs' — relief, recovery and reform.

2) To rebuild US trade and industry to help the economy to recover.

3) To create social and economic reforms that would protect future progress.

FDR was popular before the election, and he also made some popular election promises (unlike Hoover).

Roosevelt promised to act immediately after the election to fight the Depression and to take a more flexible approach.	He promised direct relief for small banks and homeowners.	He pledged to end Prohibition, since it had failed and was very unpopular (see p.14).

Hoover and Roosevelt

Have a look at these activities to see how President Hoover went about trying to resolve the Depression.

Knowledge and Understanding

1) How did each of the following policies try to tackle the impact of the Depression?

   a) Smoot-Hawley Tariff

   b) National Credit Corporation

   c) Reconstruction Finance Corporation

   d) Federal Home Loan Bank Act

2) For each of the policies in the boxes above, explain why it failed to tackle the impact of the Depression.

Interpretation

Interpretation 1

The American people were literally starved for leadership. Herbert Hoover, who had appeared to possess exceptional qualifications for the Presidency, had failed lamentably* under the stress of a major emergency... Under his hapless** Administration the prestige*** of the Presidency had dropped to an alarmingly low level and so had popular faith in our whole constitutional system.

An extract from a biography of Franklin D. Roosevelt and one of his closest advisors by Robert Sherwood, published in 1948. Sherwood was a speechwriter for FDR during his presidency.

*very badly **unfortunate ***status

1) Summarise Sherwood's views about Hoover's role in the Depression.

Interpretation 2

When business was on the road to ruin, [businessmen]... blamed [Hoover] for lack of foresight, lack of leadership, lack of even elementary* common sense. They had not been forced to put themselves unforgettably on record; he had. They were not expected to reintroduce prosperity; he was... Doubtless the Administration's campaign of optimism had been overzealous**, but Mr. Hoover's greatest mistake had been in getting himself elected for the 1928-32 term.

An extract from a book by Frederick Lewis Allen, published in 1931. Allen worked as a journalist during the 1920s, and the book contains his observations on the decade.

*basic **over-enthusiastic

2) How do Allen's views about Hoover's role in the Depression differ from Sherwood's?

3) Why do you think these interpretations give different views about Hoover's role in the Depression? Use the background information about each author to help you.

Ironically, it was Roosevelt's job to clean up Hoover's mess...

When you're facing a tricky interpretation, there are a few things you can do to make your life easier. Try tackling the interpretation one sentence at a time, underlining key words as you go.

Roosevelt and the New Deal

As soon as Roosevelt became President in March 1933, he began to introduce the New Deal he'd promised.

The First New Deal aimed to bring Relief, Recovery and Reform

1) The first period of FDR's presidency was called the 'Hundred Days'. During this time, he put a huge amount of legislation in place to help America tackle the Depression.

2) One of FDR's first acts was to restore confidence in the banking system, which had nearly collapsed by February 1933. He passed the Emergency Banking Act in March 1933 which saw the government reorganise and supervise weaker banks. Three months later, a law was introduced which made banks take steps to protect people's deposits. After these changes, fewer banks failed, deposits started to rise, and confidence in banking began to return.

> FDR attempted to get people to trust the government. His first speech as President was hopeful and determined — this boosted the population's morale. During the Hundred Days, he began friendly radio broadcasts (which became known as fireside chats) where he explained the action the government was taking. These continued throughout his presidency.

3) Roosevelt created many federal agencies (these 'alphabet agencies' were known by their initials) to fight the economic and social results of the Depression. Examples of these agencies include:

National Recovery Administration (NRA) — worked with businesses to reform working practices. It created codes for 'fair competition', set minimum wages and maximum working hours, and encouraged trade unions. This aimed to aid economic recovery.	Federal Emergency Relief Administration (FERA) — provided money for state and local governments to use for emergency relief. It funded relief payments for the unemployed and provided direct support for the poor (e.g. soup kitchens).	Civilian Conservation Corps (CCC) — provided paid labour for thousands of unemployed young men in forestry, water and soil conservation projects. By June 1942, it had given work to more than 3 million people.	Agricultural Adjustment Administration (AAA) — paid farmers to limit food production, which meant prices and incomes rose. This gave essential relief to farmers. It also reformed agriculture by helping farmers to modernise and rebuild their farms.

The Second New Deal began in 1935

The Second New Deal focused more on improving social welfare (people's health and well-being). This involved looking after the most vulnerable people in society.

1) The Social Security Act (1935) meant that Americans aged over 65 started to receive a government pension, and workers could receive unemployment benefit if they lost their job. Schemes were also set up to help the sick, the disabled and poor children.

> Before FDR, the government hadn't really interfered in people's lives and wasn't responsible for social welfare. The First New Deal gave people some direct relief, but this was only meant to be temporary. The Second New Deal was different — it did much more to improve social welfare.

2) The Wagner Act (1935) gave workers the right to join trade unions without the risk of being sacked. The National Labor Relations Board was created to step in when employers and unions disagreed. However, some workers (such as farmers) weren't covered by the act.

3) The Works Progress Administration (WPA) formed in 1935. It created work for over 8.5 million people, including jobs in construction and the arts.

4) The Farm Security Administration (FSA) was set up in 1936 (the AAA had ended in 1935). It settled families on government farms and gave them advice on farming. The FSA later helped tenant farmers apply for loans so that they could buy land.

Comment and Analysis

The Second New Deal had an important long-term effect on US society. It laid the foundations for a welfare state and changed the way that Americans saw the duties of the federal government.

The New Deal had an Impact on Social Welfare and Employment

1) Agencies like the FERA, which gave emergency relief, improved people's welfare in the short term. The Social Security Act made the social welfare of the population a long-term government concern.

2) Unemployment didn't end under the New Deal, but it did go down as a result of agencies such as the CCC and the WPA providing jobs for millions of unemployed people.

> In 1933, nearly 25% of workers were unemployed, but by 1940, unemployment had fallen to just under 15%. Also, between 1932 and 1939, farmers' incomes had doubled.

3) The New Deal didn't end the Depression, but the reforms it introduced managed to stop society and the economy from collapsing completely.

Roosevelt and the New Deal

The New Deal brought big changes to America, and these activities will help you to get to grips with them.

Knowledge and Understanding

1) Copy and complete the flowchart below by adding details about the state of America's banking system in each month.

a) February 1933 → b) March 1933 → c) June 1933

2) What were President Roosevelt's fireside chats? Why do you think he did them?

3) Copy and complete the table below by giving the full name of each agency that was created as part of the First New Deal, then explaining what each agency did.

Agency	Name	What it did
a) NRA		
b) FERA		
c) CCC		
d) AAA		

4) Copy and complete the mind map below, explaining what each aspect of the Second New Deal involved.

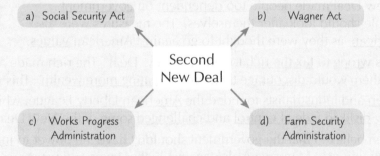

a) Social Security Act

b) Wagner Act

Second New Deal

c) Works Progress Administration

d) Farm Security Administration

5) In your own words, explain the difference between the aims of the First New Deal and the aims of the Second New Deal.

EXAM TIP

I'd like to start the No More Acronyms Alliance (NMAA)...

In the exam, don't spend too long on the questions that are only worth four marks — you need to give yourself plenty of time to answer the questions that are worth the most marks.

New Deal Opposition and Criticism

The New Deal was quite successful and had many supporters, but it still faced opposition and criticism.

Some argued that the New Deal went Against the Constitution

In the USA, power is held by the President, Congress (elected politicians) and the Supreme Court — their powers are laid down in a set of laws called the Constitution. The Constitution is very important to Americans — going against it is often seen as an attack on the American way of life.

1) Many of the Supreme Court judges were Republicans who disagreed with FDR's policies. In 1935, they used a court case to undermine FDR.

2) They said that FDR was taking power that the Constitution hadn't given to him. They declared some parts of the First New Deal unconstitutional and many of FDR's agencies (like the NRA and the AAA) were closed.

> The Supreme Court is the most powerful court in the USA. It has 9 judges who are chosen by the President and politicians. They judge cases that are linked to the Constitution and laws that apply in every state.

3) In 1937, FDR tried to add more Democrats to the Supreme Court so it would support him. He didn't ask permission to do this, which angered Congress and the Court. Eventually, the Court stopped trying to bring down existing New Deal policies and FDR backed down on his threat to change the Supreme Court.

The First New Deal didn't go Far Enough for some

1) Many people thought that FDR needed to do more to help the poor. Many of the reforms that were introduced by the First New Deal either hadn't worked or hadn't done enough to relieve poverty. Many work relief jobs were only temporary, and unemployment was still a big problem in 1934.

2) Senator Huey Long was a radical, left-wing critic of the New Deal. He wanted to tax the rich and give every family $2000 a year. He called this plan 'Share Our Wealth'. He said the families would spend the money, which would create more demand for goods and services, and therefore create more jobs.

3) Father Charles Coughlin, a popular radio host, was another radical figure who opposed the New Deal. He had supported FDR at first but later turned against him, as he thought that the government should do more to control big industries and banks. He created the National Union of Social Justice to oppose FDR.

Other Opponents said it had gone Too Far

1) Many of Roosevelt's conservative critics, including Republicans, said that he was spending too much government money on the New Deal.

2) Some said the New Deal made people too dependent on government aid and said people should look after themselves. The measures were also labelled un-American, as they were thought to go against American values.

> Many people thought that FDR had too much power — some said that he wanted to take over and rule as a dictator. FDR's attempt to appoint Supreme Court judges in 1937 made people even more worried.

3) Others said it was wrong to tax the rich to fund the New Deal. The rich made an effort to earn their wealth — taxing them would discourage them from creating more wealth. This was a capitalist view.

4) Some businessmen and industrialists founded the American Liberty League, which opposed the New Deal — they disliked federal control and challenged some of the New Deal's acts and agencies.

5) Many businessmen believed that the government shouldn't have the power to interfere in business (e.g. by supporting unions). Many were also against higher taxes and wages under the New Deal.

The New Deal Didn't Benefit Everyone

> Critics accused some New Deal programmes of 'boondoggling' — paying workers to do useless jobs just to reduce unemployment.

1) Although unemployment fell as a result of the New Deal, it didn't bring back the low unemployment levels of the 1920s. It also didn't revive industry. While production did increase, it didn't fully pick up again until World War II (see p.28).

2) African Americans faced discrimination through New Deal agencies. The CCC segregated black workers, and the NRA allowed white workers to be paid more than African Americans for doing the same job.

3) Women also gained work through the FERA and the WPA, but they too faced discrimination. New Deal programs often placed more emphasis on helping men, and women were often paid less than men.

Americans' Experiences of the Depression and New Deal

New Deal Opposition and Criticism

This page will help you to understand all of the different criticisms that Roosevelt's New Deal encountered.

Knowledge and Understanding

1) In your own words, write a short definition for each of the following key terms.

   a) Congress
   b) Constitution
   c) Supreme Court

2) Why did Roosevelt try to add more judges to the Supreme Court? Give as much detail as possible.

3) Copy and complete the table below by explaining why each group of people opposed the New Deal.

Group	Why they opposed the New Deal
a) **Supreme Court Judges**	
b) **Politicians**	
c) **Businessmen and Industrialists**	

4) In what way did New Deal agencies discriminate against the following groups?

   a) African Americans   b) Women

Thinking Historically

1) Which group of people who opposed the New Deal do you think might have concerned Roosevelt the most? Explain your answer.

Use the table above to help you to answer this question.

2) Copy and complete the mind map below by explaining the social and economic consequences of Roosevelt's New Deal during the 1930s. Use information from pages 22 and 24 to help you.

a) Social Consequences ← Consequences of the New Deal → b) Economic Consequences

3) How successful do you think the New Deal was overall? Explain your answer.

Roosevelt's New Deal really struggled to please everyone...

In the exam, use specific terminology such as 'Supreme Court'. It's a good way of showing the examiner that you've got an in-depth understanding of the topic you're writing about.

Americans' Experiences of the Depression and New Deal

1930s Popular Culture

Popular culture served different purposes in the Depression era — it often offered hope or reflected real life.

Popular Culture provided an Escape from Reality...

1) Cinema was still very popular in the 1930s. 'Talkies' (see p.8) were now an established part of the film industry, and audio in films meant that musicals became popular. They featured glamorous stars, such as Fred Astaire and Ginger Rogers, in decadent settings — this was a huge contrast to the audience's everyday lives.

2) Lots of films were made in the 1930s, and in a variety of genres — gangster films, comedies and horror films were all well received. Films such as 'The Wizard of Oz' and 'King Kong' took people into fantasy worlds far away from the reality of the Depression.

3) A lot of music was optimistic. Songs like 'We're in the Money' and 'Life Is Just a Bowl of Cherries' delivered hopeful messages to Americans. The song Roosevelt chose as his presidential campaign theme tune, 'Happy Days Are Here Again', remained extremely popular throughout the decade.

4) Band leaders like Benny Goodman popularised 'swing' music. Similar to jazz (see p.8), it was up-tempo, easy to dance to and performed in clubs in cities and towns. People could also listen to swing at home on their radios.

Fred Astaire and Ginger Rogers in the film 'Swing Time', 1936.

'Gone with the Wind', a 1939 film adaptation of a novel set during the American Civil War, had massive success. It portrayed determination to overcome war and poverty — this may have offered hope to people struggling in the 1930s. It set box office records at the time.

Some famous swing musicians, such as band leader Duke Ellington, were African-American. Bands and audiences were often segregated, but some bands did start to feature both black and white musicians by the mid-1930s.

Radios became very popular across America — they gave people access to a wide variety of entertainment such as sport, news, comedy, soap operas and music.

5) The very first superhero, Superman, appeared in a comic book in 1938 and became very popular. Comic books provided escapism — it may have been that people suffering the uncertainties of the Depression enjoyed reading about heroic figures who could overcome anything.

6) Attendance at baseball games fell as people couldn't afford tickets, and teams were forced to cut players' wages. In an attempt to encourage more fans to attend, teams started playing games at night when people weren't at work. Players like Babe Ruth and Joe DiMaggio provided excitement for those who did attend.

... but it also Reflected Life in the Depression

1) Depression-era American literature often portrayed the everyday lives of people in society who were struggling. John Steinbeck's novel, 'The Grapes of Wrath', follows a family leaving their farm in the Dust Bowl (see p.18) to find work in California. Richard Wright's 'Native Son' focuses on oppressed African Americans facing discrimination in the ghettos of Chicago.

2) Some films also portrayed the harsh reality of life in 1930s America. 'Wild Boys of the Road' follows two teenage friends whose families are suffering from the effects of unemployment — the teenagers decide to leave home to try and find work themselves. The film 'Modern Times', about a struggling factory worker, depicts widespread unemployment, poverty and homelessness in American society.

Comment and Analysis

Despite most people having far less money to spend during the Depression, aspects of popular culture, such as films, music and literature, flourished. People used popular culture to distract themselves or to directly address the issues that they were facing at the time.

Guthrie had himself fled the Dust Bowl, staying in migrant camps as he made his way to California in search of employment. His music was very political and often focused on his own personal experiences.

3) Songs like 'Brother, Can You Spare a Dime?', recorded by Bing Crosby, portrayed life for the unemployed. Blues singer Lead Belly used his songs to comment on the struggles faced by African Americans, and folk singer Woody Guthrie reflected on the hardships of Dust Bowl migrants and workers in his music.

1930s Popular Culture

Have a go at the following activities to get a better understanding of popular culture during the Depression.

Knowledge and Understanding

1) Give three examples of film genres that were popular in 1930s America.

2) In what way did musicals provide a contrast to people's everyday lives?

3) Using the following key words, explain how music developed in 1930s America.

optimistic   swing   radio

4) In what way did swing music help to promote racial equality?

5) How was baseball affected by the Depression? What did baseball teams do in response?

6) Who was Woody Guthrie? How did his experience of the Depression influence his music?

Thinking Historically

1) Copy and complete the table below. For each example of popular culture, describe what it was, then explain how it reflected life in America during the Depression. Use information from elsewhere in the book to help you.

Example	What it was	How it reflected life in America
a) 'The Grapes of Wrath'		
b) 'Native Son'		
c) 'Modern Times'		

EXAM TIP

What's your favourite type of film? Mine's cling...

When you're writing a longer exam answer, it's important to link your ideas together clearly. Use linking words and phrases like 'for example', 'therefore', 'because of this' and 'however'.

Economic Impact of World War Two

Many Americans lost their lives in World War Two, but it also had a big impact on the American economy.

The war Boosted the US Economy even Before America Joined

When the UK and France declared war on Germany in September 1939, America chose not to join the fighting. Many Americans didn't want the USA to get involved in another war, despite some of their closest allies being involved in the conflict.

1) When the Second World War broke out, America was still facing the effects of the Depression. The New Deal (see p.22) had managed to stabilise the economy, but many people were still experiencing poverty and unemployment.

When the Second World War started in 1939, 16% of Americans were still without jobs — that figure had been only 5.5% ten years earlier in 1929.

2) Although the USA chose not to fight, the government introduced the Lend-Lease programme in 1941 to help support the Allies (the countries fighting Germany). The US government bought weapons and other military supplies, such as ships and planes, from US manufacturers and sent them to the Allied armies already fighting in Europe. The majority of these goods were given to the UK and the USSR.

3) The Lend-Lease programme saw the production of war supplies increase in the USA. This helped to reduce unemployment and boost the economy before America had even entered the war.

The Lend-Lease Act gave FDR the authority to help any nation, if he believed that supporting them would help defend the USA. Although the USA didn't charge the Allies for any goods that were used up or destroyed during the war, it still benefited from sending them — the goods were produced in the USA, which stimulated American industry and, therefore, the economy.

4) The USA also exported other supplies to the Allies, such as chemicals and clothing. Raw materials, such as coal and timber, were sent to Europe too. Food was another significant export. Growing demand for food in Europe meant that American farms prospered, and agricultural production in the US rose to its highest point since 1929.

5) Farmers also benefited as demand for agricultural produce rose. By 1941, farmer's incomes were back to pre-Depression levels.

The US Economy Prospered when America Joined the war

In December 1941, Japan carried out a surprise attack on the US Navy fleet stationed at Pearl Harbor in Hawaii. Around 2400 Americans died in the attack. After this, the USA declared war on Japan, Italy and Germany, and joined the Second World War.

1) After America entered the war, the government spent lots more money to help factories cope with wartime industry. In January 1942, Roosevelt established the War Production Board (WPB) to oversee an increase in American production. The WPB helped to convert existing factories so that they could meet the demands of the war. Car factories started to build plane parts, weapons, tanks and trucks. Factories that usually made metal products like nails switched to making bullets and shells.

2) New businesses and factories were also established, as America tried to meet the needs of their armed forces, as well as continuing to support their Allies.

3) The boom in industrial production created millions of new jobs, while millions of others went to join the armed forces. This ended the mass unemployment America had faced during the Depression, and by the end of 1943, there was a shortage of workers.

The Alabama Dry Dock in the shipbuilding town of Mobile had 1000 workers in 1940. By 1943 it employed 30,000 people.

Comment and Analysis

The outbreak of the Second World War transformed the American economy. Employment levels rose dramatically and industrial production reached tremendous heights — at the time it was seen as a miracle. The war had finally achieved what Roosevelt's New Deal had set out to do.

4) There was also a shortage of agricultural workers. The war meant that there was huge demand for food from the US Army and the Allies, but many farm workers were drafted into the Army or found better paid factory jobs.

5) High employment levels, as well as the demand for workers across the country, caused wages to rise. The population now had more money to spend, and this further boosted the US economy.

Economic Impact of World War Two

The activities on this page will boost your knowledge about the economic consequences of World War Two.

Knowledge and Understanding

1) Why didn't America join the fighting when the Second World War broke out in 1939?

2) Using the following key words, describe the situation that America was in when the Second World War broke out.

Depression	stability	unemployment

3) What was the Lend-Lease programme? How did it work?

4) In what way did the Lend-Lease programme boost the US economy?

5) Give five examples of non-military supplies that America exported to the Allies at the start of the Second World War.

6) Why did America enter the Second World War in 1941?

Thinking Historically

1) Copy and complete the table below by explaining how each area of the US economy was affected by America entering the Second World War.

Area of US economy	How it was affected by entering the war
a) Production	
b) Employment	
c) Wages	

2) Do you think that the Second World War or the New Deal was more important in ending the Depression? Use information from page 28 and earlier in the section to explain your answer.

The Second World War kick-started America's economy...

The Second World War played an important role in America's economic recovery. Make sure you understand the economic impact of the war before and after America joined the fighting.

Americans' Experiences of the Depression and New Deal

Social Impact of World War Two

Women made a big contribution to the war effort by working in factories and joining the military. This helped them gain more independence and fight gender stereotypes — but they still faced discrimination.

Women were Limited to Certain Jobs before the war

1) Before the war started, the number of women in the workforce had been growing. The Depression (see p.18) had caused many men to lose their jobs, which meant they were no longer able to support their families. This rising poverty forced both men and women to look for work.

2) However, most women were paid less than men and were limited to working in typically 'female' jobs, such as teaching, nursing and cleaning. Working women were criticised during the Depression for taking jobs away from men, and even New Deal relief programs discriminated against women (see p.24).

Thousands of Women joined Military Services

1) During the war, many women joined the military in non-fighting roles, which freed up men to fight.

The WAVES was a Navy Corps	The WASPS helped the Air Force	The WAC was part of the Army
The WAVES replaced Navy officers and seamen who had shore roles. They worked in all sorts of roles, including as engineers, doctors and radio operators.	The WASPS were pilots. They were never officially part of the military, but they flew Air Force planes in non-combat roles in the USA, which freed up male pilots to fight.	The WAC included mechanics, typists, switchboard operators and office clerks. Around 150,000 women had served in the Corps by the end of the war.

2) Female activists had to campaign to get these groups created. They didn't have much support from military authorities — many didn't like women being in the military.

3) In 1943, recruitment to the WAC suffered, because women who joined the Corps were wrongly accused of being immoral. These rumours were mainly spread by people who didn't want women doing jobs that were traditionally reserved for men.

Comment and Analysis

Women still faced sexism after the war, but these groups showed that people were wrong to think women couldn't handle jobs usually done by men.

Millions of Women were employed in the War Effort

1) During the war, millions of factory jobs became vacant when men were drafted into the Army. Lots of new jobs were also created in defence work.

2) The government started a propaganda campaign to get women to join the war effort and enter the workforce. It featured the character 'Rosie the Riveter'.

3) Millions of women did skilled jobs in factories, shipyards and defence facilities. For example, some worked as plane engineers and mechanics at Brookley Field.

4) Lots of women volunteered to work on farms in the Woman's Land Army (WLA).

A poster of 'Rosie the Riveter'. This campaign boosted the morale of female workers and encouraged others to join in.

During the war, millions of women earned their own money and did jobs that they didn't normally do (e.g. butchers). Many young women moved out of their family home to find work, so they had more freedom in their social lives. Many didn't want to be dependent on their families or husbands again after the war.

5) Despite women gaining new jobs in wartime, they still faced discrimination — they were often paid less than men for doing the same jobs during the war.

6) When the war ended, women were widely expected to stop working and go back to their domestic roles. Many of them lost their jobs as they were replaced by the millions of men returning home from the war.

By the early 1950s, the number of women with jobs had increased again — many still wanted to work. However, those jobs were most often as secretaries, clerical workers or teachers. Fewer women worked in industry — 'Rosie the Riveter' was a far less accurate representation of women after the war.

Social Impact of World War Two

Have a go at the activities on this page to get a better idea of how the Second World War affected women.

Knowledge and Understanding

1) Why were more women working before the Second World War broke out? What difficulties did women in the workforce face?

2) Copy and complete the mind map below by describing how women in each group contributed to the war effort.

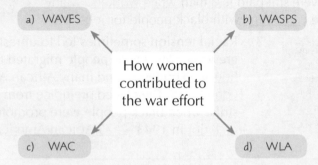

a) WAVES

b) WASPS

How women contributed to the war effort

c) WAC

d) WLA

Interpretation

The interpretation below is from an interview with Dellie Hahne in the 1980s. Hahne worked as a nurse's assistant during the Second World War, which started not long after she had left university.

> They were hammering away that the woman who went to work did it temporarily to help her man, and when he came back, he took her job and she cheerfully leaped back to the home... I think a lot of women said, "Screw that noise". 'Cause they had a taste of freedom, they had a taste of making their own money, a taste of spending their own money, making their own decisions. I think the beginning of the women's movement had its seeds right there in World War Two.

1) Summarise Hahne's views on each of the following points. For each point, give one detail from the interpretation to support your answer.

a) How women were expected to behave at the end of the war.

b) How women responded to these expectations of them.

c) The long-term significance of World War Two for women.

2) Do you think that the interpretation is convincing about women's attitudes towards work at the end of the Second World War? Use information from page 30 to explain your answer.

There was still a long way to go to reach gender equality...

When you're writing about how convincing interpretations are, don't comment on the authors' backgrounds. Instead, use your own knowledge of the topic to back up each point you make.

Social Impact of World War Two

The Civil Rights movement of the 1950s and 1960s was based on gains that were made during the war.

Roosevelt banned Racial Discrimination in Defence Industries

1) In June 1941, President Roosevelt signed Executive Order 8802, which formed the Fair Employment Practice Committee and made it illegal to discriminate against defence workers because of their race. He didn't want anything to get in the way of the war effort.

2) After this, thousands of African Americans migrated to northern cities to find work in war production, and this created racial tension. African Americans were paid more in the North than they had been in the South, but they were still paid less than white workers. Many white people didn't like competing with black people for jobs.

> Civil Rights campaigners had threatened to stage massive protests in Washington if defence jobs weren't opened up for African Americans. Roosevelt wanted to prevent the disruption and international embarrassment this would cause.

> Some companies (like the Alabama Dry Dock) segregated workers, while others allowed white and black Americans to work together. This was unusual, since segregation was still in place in the rest of society.

3) Racial tension sometimes led to unrest. In Detroit, the population grew very quickly as people migrated there for war work. There were housing shortages, and many African Americans had to live in poor conditions. They faced prejudice from white workers, who went on strike when black people were promoted. These tensions caused a race riot in 1943 — 25 African Americans and 9 white people died.

Black Americans campaigned for Victory in the War and at Home

1) During the war, many black Americans questioned why they should fight for freedoms for Europeans that the USA didn't give to them — they faced segregation and racist discrimination. Civil Rights activists created a campaign called 'Double Victory', which urged black people to fight for democracy in Europe and to fight for their own democratic rights at home in the USA.

2) CORE (Congress of Racial Equality) was founded in 1942. It was strongly influenced by Mahatma Gandhi's philosophy of non-violence, and was dedicated to non-violent protest.

> During the war, the letter V was used as a symbol for victory over oppression. It was then adopted by African Americans to symbolise their fight for a double victory — one victory against enemies from outside America (like Hitler) and another victory over people inside America who wanted to deny rights to African Americans.

3) CORE protested against segregation in American society. In 1943, it staged one of the first sit-in protests (see p.46) to try and desegregate a Chicago restaurant.

4) The protest methods of CORE set the foundations of the Civil Rights movement in the 1950s and 1960s — their non-violent message was echoed by future Civil Rights leaders like Martin Luther King (see p.48).

Truman ended Segregation in the Army in 1948

Before the war, the US Army had a policy called 'segregation without discrimination'. They thought the Army worked better when black and white soldiers were separated.

> This was similar to the idea of 'separate but equal' (see p.44). The Army was nicknamed the 'Jim Crow Army' by Civil Rights activists.

1) African Americans enlisted in large numbers during the war, but suffered segregation. They had worse training and worse working and living conditions. They were often stuck in non-combat units, doing things like building roads and transporting supplies.

> Despite continued segregation, many African Americans served with distinction during the war. One example is the Tuskegee Airmen — an all-black unit of pilots and other aircraft operators. They flew in hundreds of missions and gained a reputation for bravery.

2) A law was passed in 1940 that made it illegal to discriminate against black men in army recruitment, but there were still limits on how many black men could enlist and segregation continued.

3) The government debated whether to end army segregation during the war — leisure facilities were desegregated in 1943 and army transport buses in 1944, but the segregation of soldiers continued.

4) In 1946, black men were banned from enlisting. Civil Rights activists asked the government to reverse this.

5) In 1948, American Civil Rights activists protested against segregation. President Truman supported desegregation in the Army, and in July 1948 he signed Executive Order 9981, which made this law.

Social Impact of World War Two

The activities on this page will help you get to grips with the impact of World War Two on African Americans.

Knowledge and Understanding

1) What was Executive Order 8802? Why did Roosevelt agree to sign it?

2) Why did some African Americans start to question whether they should take part in the fighting during the Second World War?

3) In your own words, write a short definition for each of the following key terms.

   a) Double Victory
   b) CORE

4) In what way did CORE influence the Civil Rights movement in the 1950s and 1960s?

5) Copy and complete the timeline below, adding the key events in the development of desegregation in the Army.

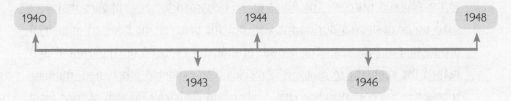

Thinking Historically

1) The flowchart below shows the development of racial tension in the defence industry. Copy and complete the flowchart, adding the consequence of each event or development. Give as much detail as possible.

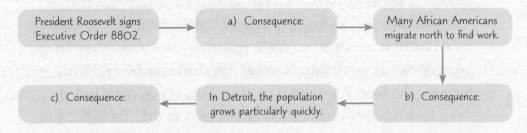

2) In what way did the Army's policy of 'segregation without discrimination' fail? Explain your answer.

Revise this stuff and you'll be victorious in the exam...

If you're struggling to understand the causes or consequences of a particular event, drawing a flowchart might help you. It's a fantastic way to make sense of how one thing led to another.

Worked Exam-Style Question

Take a look at the sample answer below, which will help you to tackle the 12-mark question in the exam.

Look at the bullet points below. Which one was more important for America?

- economic consequences of the Second World War
- social consequences of the Second World War

Explain your answer, referring to both bullet points.   [12 marks]

The Second World War had significant economic and social consequences for America, but overall, the economic consequences were more important.

One economic consequence of the Second World War was that it boosted US industry and agriculture. When the war broke out in 1939, America was still suffering from the consequences of the Depression. However, the demands of the war in Europe helped to solve America's economic problems before it even joined the war. In 1941, Lend-Lease was introduced, which saw the government buy military supplies from US manufacturers and send them to the Allies in Europe. The Allies weren't charged for any supplies that were used up or destroyed during the war, but the programme boosted industrial production in America. The growth of industry reduced unemployment and helped the economy to recover. America also exported other, non-military supplies to Europe, including coal, timber and chemicals, as well as food from US farms. The growing demand for food in Europe meant that US farms prospered, as agricultural production reached its highest point since 1929 and farmers' incomes returned to pre-Depression levels. This shows that the demands of the war played an important role in rescuing America's economy.

The economic consequences of the Second World War continued to benefit America after it joined the war in 1941. The US armed forces needed military supplies as well as the Allies in Europe, meaning that industry had to expand. The government invested heavily in industry, and created the War Production Board (WPB) to oversee an increase in production. New factories were set up, and existing ones were converted so that they could manufacture military supplies. This boom in production created millions of jobs, and helped to bring the mass unemployment of the Depression to an end. The high rate of employment and high demand for workers across the country caused wages to increase, giving people more money to spend. This added further to America's economic recovery as the war progressed.

The Second World War had a wide range of social consequences for African Americans. For example, the signing of Executive Order 8802 in 1941 opened up jobs in the defence industry to African Americans. Meanwhile, the

> This gives a basic answer to the question as an introduction.

> This links the point back to the question by explaining why these consequences were important.

> Use relevant examples to back up your point.

> It's really important to write about both of the bullet points in your answer.

Americans' Experiences of the Depression and New Deal

Worked Exam-Style Question

government introduced measures to tackle discrimination in the armed forces. A law was passed in 1940 making it illegal to discriminate against black men in army recruitment, which was followed by the desegregation of army leisure facilities and transport buses in 1943 and 1944. By 1948, after campaigning by Civil Rights activists, Truman agreed to desegregate the US Army completely. The war had other long-term consequences for African Americans, as the wartime actions of groups such as CORE helped to inspire the Civil Rights movement of the 1950s and 1960s. CORE protested against segregation using a non-violent philosophy that was echoed by people like Martin Luther King, and its methods (e.g. sit-ins) were used to desegregate public facilities in the 1950s and 1960s. However, despite the progress made by African Americans during the war, social attitudes towards them were a lot slower to change. For example, black defence workers faced hostility from white workers, who didn't want to compete with them for jobs, which led to tension and even race riots in cities like Detroit. This suggests that, although the war had positive social consequences for African Americans, prejudice and discrimination remained.

Another social consequence of the Second World War was that it gave new opportunities to women. Millions of women were allowed to join the workforce as men went to fight abroad, often in jobs that hadn't been accessible to them before. An increase in demand for military supplies, as well as a shortage of workers, meant that women were needed to work in factories, shipyards and defence facilities. Some women worked on farms as part of the WLA, while others were able to support the military in non-combat roles in the WAC, the WAVES and the WASPS. Women who worked became more independent, because they earned their own money and often had to leave the family home. However, many of them were paid less than men, and were expected to give up their jobs to returning soldiers at the end of the war. Some women continued to work after the war, but they were once again limited to typically 'female' jobs like teaching or clerical work. This suggests that the social consequences of the war for women were limited and short-term.

Overall, the economic consequences of the Second World War were more important for America than the social consequences. The social changes that African Americans and women experienced were limited by the fact that they still suffered from prejudice, and some changes were completely undone after the war ended. In contrast, the war transformed the US economy. The demands of the war boosted industry and agriculture, ending mass unemployment and giving Americans more money to spend. These changes helped America to recover from the Depression at last.

Including specific details, like names and dates, shows good knowledge of the topic.

Use specific evidence to support your argument.

Develop your argument by explaining the impact of the consequences you have discussed.

Make sure you give a clear answer to the question in the conclusion.

The conclusion sums up the points that have been made in the answer and makes an overall judgement about what was more important.

Exam-Style Questions

Now that you've worked your way through the section, it's time to have a go at some exam-style questions.

Interpretation 1

The interpretation below is from an interview with David Kennedy, published in 1970. Kennedy worked for America's central bank in the 1930s and 1940s, and went on to work in the US Treasury (the government department in charge of the economy) for Republican President Richard Nixon from 1969 to 1971.

> Roosevelt... started many things going, but they were turned on and off. We had the NRA*, the WPA* and these things — they'd come and go. You never could get clear-cut decisions. One day, one thing; the next day, another. It was bedlam** and confusion in Washington... I was enthusiastic when Roosevelt came in. I thought: We're in serious trouble. Something has to be done, and here's a man that's going to do it. I voted for him his first term and his second***. After that, I voted against him... we were not making the progress I thought our country was capable of making... I became terribly disenchanted****. He was a dramatic leader. He had charm, personality, poise and so on. He could inspire people. But to me, he lacked the stick-to-it-iveness to carry a program through.

*see p.22   **chaos

***Franklin D. Roosevelt served four terms as US President — 1933-1937, 1937-1941, 1941-1945 and January 1945 until his death in April 1945.   ****disappointed

Interpretation 2

The interpretation below is from Eleanor Roosevelt's autobiography, published in 1949. As President Roosevelt's wife, Eleanor Roosevelt was First Lady of the USA from 1933 to 1945. She was very politically active, and sometimes travelled the country to report back to FDR on public opinion and the progress of his policies.

> In my travels around the country I saw many things built both by PWA* and by CWA*. I also saw the results of the work done by CCC**. The achievements of these agencies began to dot city and rural areas alike. Soil conservation and forestry work went forward, recreation areas were built, and innumerable bridges, schools, hospitals and sanitation projects were constructed — lasting monuments to the good work done under these agencies. It is true they cost the people of the country vast sums of money, but they did a collective good and left tangible*** results which are still evident today... They pulled the country out of the depression and made it possible for us to fight the greatest and most expensive war in our history.

*Public Works Administration and Civil Works Administration — 'alphabet agencies' established to help the economy to recover and reduce unemployment by creating jobs on public works projects.

**see p.22   ***able to be seen or felt

Exam-Style Questions

Exam-Style Questions

1) Look at Interpretation 1 and Interpretation 2. In what ways do the authors' views differ about the impact of the New Deal? Use both interpretations to explain your answer.   [4 marks]

2) Explain why the authors of Interpretation 1 and Interpretation 2 might have different views about the impact of the New Deal. Use both interpretations and your own knowledge in your answer.   [4 marks]

3) Do you think Interpretation 1 or Interpretation 2 is more convincing about the impact of the New Deal? Use both interpretations and your own knowledge to explain your answer.   [8 marks]

4) Describe two difficulties that the Republican Party faced as a result of opposition to its policies in the early 1930s.   [4 marks]

5) Explain how the lives of Americans were affected by the American war effort during World War Two.   [8 marks]

6) Look at the bullet points below. Which one was more important for America between 1929 and 1939?

   • social consequences of the Depression
   • economic consequences of the Depression

   Explain your answer, referring to both bullet points.   [12 marks]

Post-War Prosperity

The strength of the post-war US economy meant that the American Dream — the belief that any person has an equal opportunity to gain wealth and success through hard work — became more achievable for some.

The Post-War Economy was Booming

1) The US economy had thrived during the Second World War (see p.28). Increased wages and levels of employment meant that many Americans were wealthier than ever before in the post-war period. Industries prospered after the war, which meant that the USA was producing a lot of goods.

2) This helped to create a rise in consumerism. There were lots of things available to buy, like fridges and dishwashers, and more people could afford them. Demand for these goods further boosted the economy.

Comment and Analysis
This prosperity was a welcome contrast to the poverty and hardships many experienced as a result of the Depression.

3) In 1944, Roosevelt had introduced the Servicemen's Readjustment Act (otherwise known as the 'G.I. Bill'). It offered veterans free college tuition, and loans to help them buy a home. By 1956, just under 10 million veterans were aided by the bill, but many black veterans were excluded from its benefits.

4) The Cold War (see p.42) led to an increase in military spending. As tensions grew, the USA invested in new industries, such as nuclear technology and space exploration and research, which created new jobs.

Prosperity Changed American Society

1) Wages continued to increase after the war up until the 1970s. This meant that people could afford a much higher standard of living than before. Many Americans became 'middle class'.

2) As veterans returned home and more people were becoming wealthy enough to support a family, the population experienced a 'baby boom'. The birth rate increased dramatically, and between 1945 and 1950, the American population grew by over 12 million.

Levittown in New York was one of the first purpose-built suburbs. It contained over 17,400 mass-produced houses.

3) A house-building boom also took place, as demand for housing grew. Low housing costs and money from the G.I. Bill meant more people could afford homes — but black veterans were often refused mortgages.

4) Many of these new houses were built in the suburbs — huge housing estates on the edges of cities and towns. These houses appealed to many Americans, and the population of both rural areas and cities declined as people moved to live in these purpose-built homes. The popularity of the suburbs reflected a rise in car ownership — people no longer needed to live close to their place of work.

5) The growth of suburbia led to impressive shopping malls being built in the suburbs. They gave people an accessible place to both shop and socialise, and soon became an important part of post-war American culture.

Many American families aspired to 'suburbia' — a comfortable life where the husband drove to work in the city from their house in the suburbs, while the wife looked after the home, using all the latest household appliances.

6) The growing population, rising wages and the birth of shopping malls all helped to encourage the post-war 'consumer boom'. More and more people were buying luxury goods like cars, record players and televisions. Television adverts became more widespread and were very influential.

The American Dream was now a Reality for Some

1) The American Dream had come true for a large part of the population. Many Americans were financially secure, had access to consumer goods, and could raise their families away from crowded, 'unsafe' cities.

2) For others, the American Dream was an illusion. Outside 'suburbia', around 25% of the population was still living in poverty — African Americans in inner-city neighbourhoods, and white communities in rural areas like Appalachia were particularly hard hit. Segregation (see p.44) and prejudice still denied African Americans equal opportunity, and women were encouraged not to seek employment — they were expected to be suburban housewives instead, which reinforced more traditional gender roles.

3) Some people didn't embrace the American Dream. They were concerned about the effect of consumerism on society, and frustrated by the conformity and traditional values of 'suburbia'.

Post-War Prosperity

Try these activities on why America was prosperous after the war, and how prosperity affected people's lives.

Knowledge and Understanding

1) Using the following key words, describe the state of America's economy during the post-war period.

   Second World War   wages   employment   industry   Cold War

2) What was the Servicemen's Readjustment Act?

Thinking Historically

1) In your own words, explain how Americans' lives were affected by each of the following post-war developments. Give as much detail as possible.

   a) Consumerism   b) Suburbia   c) Shopping Malls

Interpretation

The interpretation below is from a study of poverty in America by Michael Harrington, published in 1962. Harrington was a writer, professor and political activist who criticised capitalism for creating inequality. He is describing a 'transformation' that took place in America's cities during the 1950s.

> Now the American city has been transformed. The poor still inhabit the miserable housing in the central area, but they are increasingly isolated from contact with, or sight of, anybody else. Middle-class women coming in from Suburbia on a rare trip may catch the merest glimpse of the other America on the way to an evening at the theater, but their children are segregated in suburban schools... The failures, the unskilled, the disabled, the aged, and the minorities are right there, across the tracks, where they have always been. But hardly anyone else is.

1) Summarise Harrington's views about post-war prosperity in America.

2) Why do you think Harrington gives these views about post-war prosperity? Use the background information about Harrington to explain your answer.

3) Overall, do you think the interpretation is convincing about post-war prosperity in America? Explain your answer, using information from page 38 to help you.

The G.I. Bill comes right after the G.I. Dessert...

In the exam, you'll need to suggest reasons why two authors might express different views. Don't forget to think about the identity of each author and the purpose of each of the texts.

Post-War Popular Culture

Television and rock and roll were both major developments in popular culture in post-war USA. At this time, popular culture often highlighted the contrasting views of different generations in America.

Economic Prosperity made Popular Culture more Accessible

1) The strength of the American economy after the Second World War (see p.38) meant that people had more money to spend on different elements of popular culture.

2) New technology, such as television, led to entertainment becoming more accessible than ever before.

> On average, people had five times as much money to spend on things like music, cinema and fashion in 1955 as in 1940.

3) People who had grown up during the Depression now had families. They wanted to enjoy their new affluent society and make sure that their children had access to everything they hadn't had themselves.

Some Popular Culture presented the Ideal American Society

1) Post-war American society was built around the 'traditional' family. People were encouraged to marry early and have children, and women were mainly seen as wives and mothers who stayed at home. Families were expected to hold American values, such as patriotism, faith and morality.

2) These values were both encouraged and reflected by popular culture. TV programmes like 'Leave it to Beaver' and 'Father Knows Best' portrayed idealised and wholesome American families.

> The popularity of cinema declined as more families bought televisions. Sales rose sharply throughout the 1950s, and by 1960 around 50 million households owned a TV. Watching the same shows encouraged the population to conform to the same values.

3) Popular culture reflected traditional values partly because of fears over communism (see p.42) — people felt that the American way of life had to be protected from the communist threat. Hollywood responded by making traditional films, such as westerns and musicals, that conformed to American ideals.

> Filmmakers often avoided difficult or controversial topics to prevent suspicion that they were communists trying to undermine US society.

Popular Culture helped to create a Generation Gap

1) Many young people (who became known as 'teenagers' in the post-war period) began to rebel against conformity and adult authority in society. Teenagers had more money and free time than before, which helped them create their own distinct culture — one that was very different to previous generations.

2) An exciting new genre of music called rock and roll emerged. It was designed to appeal to young people and encouraged freedom and defiance. Rock and roll quickly became extremely popular.

- Rock and roll developed from the blues and country music. It was energetic, loud and aggressive.

- The genre originated in black culture, but was enjoyed by black and white people alike. This gave African-American stars, such as Little Richard and Chuck Berry, mainstream success.

- In 1956, Elvis Presley rose to become the icon of rock and roll. He was well-known for his good looks, suggestive dancing and daring lyrics.

- Many in society, especially parents, politicians and religious figures, were outraged by rock and roll. They thought that it encouraged behaviour amongst teenagers, such as sex, rebellion and crime, that went against American values. It was labelled 'the Devil's music'.

© Michael Ochs Archives / Stringer / Michael Ochs Archives / Getty Images

> The actor James Dean starred in 'Rebel Without a Cause'. Like Elvis, he became an icon of the post-war generation. Many young people identified with his frustrated persona and disregard for authority in the characters that he played. Adults, however, did not see Dean as a suitable role model for young people.

3) Throughout the post-war era, films which reflected rock and roll culture, like 'Rebel Without a Cause', 'The Wild One' and 'Blackboard Jungle' were released.

4) These films portray teenagers who are angry at older figures of authority or society, so rebel against them. Young Americans embraced these stories and the characters within them.

Post-War Popular Culture

US popular culture experienced some dramatic changes during the post-war period. These activities will help you to understand why these changes happened and what effect they had on people's lives.

Knowledge and Understanding

1) Give two ways in which popular culture became more accessible to people in the post-war period.

2) How was a 'traditional' family expected to behave in the post-war period? Give as much detail as possible.

3) How did fear of communism affect the way that films and TV programmes were made in post-war America?

4) What was rock and roll? Who was it meant to appeal to?

5) Who were the following people? For each one, explain why different people might have had contrasting views about them.

   a) Elvis Presley   b) James Dean

Thinking Historically

1) Copy and complete the mind map below, explaining the effects of television on post-war American society. Use information from pages 38 and 40 to help you.

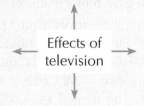

Effects of television

2) Why do you think a separate 'teenage' culture developed in the 1950s?

3) Explain why older generations might have opposed the development of a separate 'teenage' culture in the 1950s. Give as much detail as possible.

EXAM TIP

From swing music and radio to rock and roll and TV...

Make sure you understand how popular culture changed between 1920 and 1973 in America. These changes often reflect changes in society, such as the development of a generation gap.

McCarthyism

In the 1950s, a senator called Joseph McCarthy investigated possible communists in the US government. His anti-communist campaign wasn't based on reliable evidence, and it became known as McCarthyism.

Americans saw Communism as a threat at Home and Abroad

1) From around the end of the Second World War in 1945, people in the USA were becoming more and more worried about the USSR. The two countries were ideologically opposed to each other:

> The USA was capitalist. It had a democratically elected government, and its economy was based on private ownership of property, free competition and forces of supply and demand.

> The USSR was communist. It was a single-party state, and its economy was controlled by the government, with no private ownership of property.

2) Rising tension between the USA and the USSR led to a Cold War from 1945 to 1991. At this time, a climate of fear and panic started to grow in the USA — another Red Scare had begun (see p.12).

3) In the late 1940s, communism seemed to be spreading in countries around the world and becoming more powerful. The USA feared that the USSR wanted world domination.

- In the aftermath of the Second World War, the USSR developed a sphere of influence in Eastern Europe. Most Eastern European countries had communist governments installed by the USSR.
- In 1950, communist North Korea invaded non-communist South Korea. This led to the Korean War (1950-53) — the USA sent troops to Korea to try and stop the spread of communism.

4) Some politicians feared that communism was also a threat within the USA. They thought that communists were hostile to American values and that they wanted to destroy American capitalism and society.

5) There was a growing fear that, if communists were allowed to work for the American government, they would try to undermine it from the inside.

McCarthy increased Fear of Communism in the USA

1) In 1950, Senator Joseph McCarthy gave a speech during which he waved what he claimed was a list of 205 communists in the State Department (the US Foreign Office). He claimed some were putting America at risk by giving information to the USSR.

> McCarthy's anti-communist stance made him popular with voters, and this increased his political power.

2) No one else ever saw the list, but many people believed McCarthy. His claims received huge media attention, which gave him a platform to make more accusations.

3) McCarthy was involved in Senate committees investigating possible communists in the US government. At hearings, he made accusations with little evidence, intimidated witnesses and pressured people to accuse others. He destroyed the careers and reputations of thousands of people.

4) People became more fearful of communism — McCarthy's accusations made it seem like communism really was a serious threat to the USA. This fuelled anti-communism and helped create an atmosphere of hysteria. People who criticised McCarthy risked accusations that they were communist sympathisers.

5) However, some did speak out. In 1950, a group of Republican senators, led by Margaret Chase Smith, condemned McCarthy's tactics (although they didn't directly criticise McCarthy himself).

6) As it became clear that McCarthy's investigations had found very little evidence of communist activity, criticism of McCarthy became stronger and public opinion turned against him. This led to his downfall:

- The TV journalist Edward Murrow used his documentary series 'See It Now' to criticise McCarthy. An episode which aired in 1954 condemned McCarthy's tactics and argued that his 'witch-hunts' were a greater threat to US society than communism.
- In 1954, the Army-McCarthy hearings were held to investigate communism in the US Army. McCarthy's bullying of witnesses during these televised hearings made him unpopular with the public. In December 1954, the Senate voted to censure him (express strong disapproval of him).

McCarthyism

McCarthy's investigations added to the climate of fear and hysteria during the Cold War. Have a go at the activities below to get a better understanding on how this affected parts of American society.

Knowledge and Understanding

1) In what way were America and the USSR 'ideologically opposed' to each other?

2) Using the following key words, explain why there was a climate of fear in America at around the end of the Second World War.

Cold War   Eastern Europe   Korea

3) Why did some US politicians view communism as a threat to America?

4) In your own words, explain what Senator Joseph McCarthy claimed in a speech about the US State Department in 1950.

5) How did McCarthy's anti-communist stance affect his political power?

6) Give three methods that McCarthy used during his investigations.

7) Why might some people have been reluctant to criticise McCarthy?

Thinking Historically

1) Copy and complete the flowchart below by explaining how each event helped to cause McCarthy's downfall.

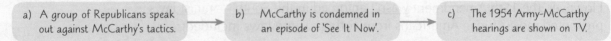

a) A group of Republicans speak out against McCarthy's tactics. → b) McCarthy is condemned in an episode of 'See It Now'. → c) The 1954 Army-McCarthy hearings are shown on TV.

2) Which event do you think was most significant in causing McCarthy's downfall? Explain your answer, using the flowchart above to help you.

McCarthy's witch-hunts didn't find many witches...

It's useful to know what caused McCarthy's rise and fall. Make sure you know the order of all the key events, the names of all the key figures and the roles these figures played.

Segregation

Black Americans and white Americans were <u>segregated</u> by law in the South — this meant that they had to use <u>separate facilities</u>. The facilities for black Americans were often <u>inferior</u>, which <u>denied</u> them <u>equality</u>.

Jim Crow Laws enforced Segregation in the South

1) <u>Segregation</u> was legally enforced by <u>Jim Crow Laws</u>, which were introduced throughout the South from the <u>late 19th century</u>.

2) Workplaces, schools, public transport, parks, beaches and swimming pools were all <u>segregated</u>, as were restaurants, drinking fountains and public toilets.

3) Facilities for white people and African Americans were supposed to be '<u>separate but equal</u>', but the ones provided for black people were usually <u>much worse</u>.

This bus station had segregated waiting rooms. One of the signs reads 'colored waiting room'.

The '<u>separate but equal</u>' doctrine was created in 1890 to <u>justify racial segregation</u>. This policy was often <u>ignored</u> and Jim Crow Laws were used to <u>deny equality</u> to African Americans. Many black people were <u>forced</u> to live as <u>second-class citizens</u>.

Segregation limited Opportunities for African Americans

1) <u>Education</u> was segregated in the South, with <u>separate schools</u> for white and black students. This made it <u>difficult</u> for African-American children to get a <u>good education</u>. Schools for African Americans relied on white-controlled local governments for their funding, so they received far <u>less money</u> than white schools. As a result, most African-American schools were <u>overcrowded</u>, had <u>poor quality buildings</u> and <u>lacked books</u> and other resources.

2) In the South, most African Americans worked as <u>farm labourers</u>. Their employment opportunities outside of farming were limited because they were <u>barred</u> from <u>skilled jobs</u> in industry and from most <u>professional</u> and <u>office jobs</u>.

The majority of African Americans didn't complete secondary school — in the late 1930s, only <u>19%</u> of African Americans aged 14-17 were enrolled in <u>high school</u>.

In the <u>North</u>, there were no Jim Crow Laws, but black people still faced discrimination, especially in <u>employment</u> and <u>housing</u>. For example, <u>homeowners' associations</u> discouraged selling houses in white communities to African Americans, which limited black people to <u>run-down</u> and <u>overcrowded</u> neighbourhoods. African Americans were also often restricted to <u>unskilled jobs</u> which were <u>badly paid</u>.

Most African Americans in the South were Unable to Vote

1) The <u>15th Amendment</u> to the US Constitution was introduced in 1870. It says that no US citizen should be denied the <u>right to vote</u> because of their <u>race</u> or <u>colour</u>.

2) However, the 15th Amendment <u>wasn't enforced</u> in the <u>South</u> — racist laws prevented most African Americans from voting. These laws included:

- <u>Poll taxes</u>, which voters had to pay in order to vote. Many poor African Americans couldn't afford to pay.

- <u>Property requirements</u> — only those who owned property over a certain value could vote. Few African Americans owned such properties.

- <u>Literacy or understanding tests</u> — African Americans rarely passed, because the tests were carried out by white officials who deliberately failed black entrants.

Comment and Analysis

These laws meant that African Americans living in the South had <u>no voice</u> in politics. As a result, <u>state governments</u> in the South were dominated by the <u>Democratic Party</u>, which <u>supported segregation</u>. These southern Democrats were also <u>powerful</u> in the <u>federal (national) government</u> and, along with many Republicans, <u>blocked</u> attempts to get rid of segregation and give African Americans <u>equal rights</u>.

3) The laws preventing African Americans from voting also <u>stopped</u> them serving on <u>juries</u>. This made it very <u>difficult</u> for an African-American defendant to get a <u>fair trial</u> in a southern court.

Segregation

African Americans suffered under Jim Crow Laws in the South. This page will make sure you know what these laws were and how the lives of African Americans in the South were affected by them.

Knowledge and Understanding

1) Write a short definition for each of the following key terms.

   a) Jim Crow Laws   b) 'Separate But Equal'

2) Explain what the 15th Amendment is.

3) Copy and complete the table below, explaining how each law prevented African Americans in the South from voting.

Law	How it prevented African Americans from voting
a) **Poll Taxes**	
b) **Property Requirements**	
c) **Literacy Tests**	

4) The laws preventing African Americans from voting also prevented them from serving on juries. How did this affect African Americans?

5) In the North, what discrimination did African Americans face in each of the following areas?

   a) Housing   b) Employment

Thinking Historically

1) Copy and complete the mind map below by explaining why African Americans in the South faced difficulties in each area.

   a) Education ← African Americans in the South → b) Employment

   c) Politics

African Americans were treated as second-class citizens...

Be specific when you're explaining how people's lives were affected by a factor or an event. Consider how different groups were affected and how the effects changed as time went on.

The Civil Rights Movement

Civil Rights activists protested against segregation in the South and were often successful in changing laws.

The Supreme Court ruled against Segregated Education

1) The US Supreme Court is the highest court in the USA. It has the final say on whether state and federal laws obey the Constitution.

2) Following campaigns by the NAACP, the Supreme Court ruled in the case Brown v Board of Education of Topeka (1954) that racial segregation in schools was unconstitutional (went against the US Constitution). This meant that southern states were supposed to desegregate their public schools.

> The NAACP (National Association for the Advancement of Colored People) aimed to ensure equality for all. It funded several important court cases challenging discrimination.

3) The Brown v Board of Education ruling weakened the legal basis for the southern states' Jim Crow Laws and segregation. It also inspired activists to challenge discrimination in other areas of life.

> However, there was strong opposition to the desegregation of public schools — state authorities often tried to defy the Supreme Court's ruling. Also, the lack of a national Civil Rights law meant that it was difficult for the federal government to enforce desegregation in individual states. This caused problems such as those seen in Little Rock, Arkansas in 1957. Nine African-American students were enrolled at Central High School in Little Rock, but on their first day they were met by an angry mob. The state governor, Orval Faubus, sent the National Guard (soldiers controlled by the state) to keep the black students out. President Eisenhower intervened and sent in US Army troops to enforce desegregation. These problems continued into the 1960s. In 1963, Governor Wallace blocked black students from enrolling at the University of Alabama. President Kennedy took control of the Alabama National Guard and ordered them to ensure that the students were admitted.

Civil Rights protesters Successfully Challenged segregation

Activists staged non-violent protests against segregation, which received lots of media coverage. This helped raise awareness of racial discrimination in the South and win public support for the Civil Rights movement.

The Montgomery Bus Boycott (1955)

- Rosa Parks was a member of the NAACP and a committed Civil Rights activist. In 1955, she was arrested for refusing to give up her bus seat to a white passenger in Montgomery, Alabama.
- Black ministers, led by Martin Luther King (see p.48), organised a bus boycott in protest. For more than a year, African Americans supported the boycott by walking to work or sharing cars. During the boycott, protesters were violently attacked, and four churches and King's home were bombed.
- The Supreme Court eventually ruled that Alabama's bus segregation laws were unconstitutional. The success of this peaceful protest was inspirational to all who opposed segregation in the South.

The Greensboro Sit-Ins (1960)

- In February 1960, a group of black and white college students staged sit-ins at the segregated lunch counter in the Woolworths department store in Greensboro, North Carolina. The protests continued for several months and were eventually successful — the counter was desegregated in July 1960.
- The sit-ins quickly spread throughout the country. It's estimated that more than 50,000 students had participated in a sit-in by April 1960. These protests were often successful in forcing desegregation.
- Police officers and other government officials sometimes used force to remove protesters.

The Freedom Rides (1961)

- In 1961, protesters began to challenge segregation on interstate bus services. Groups of African Americans and white Americans boarded interstate buses in the North (where they were desegregated) and travelled together to southern states that enforced segregation.
- When they reached the South, protesters were often attacked by violent mobs or arrested by local authorities. The widespread violence forced President Kennedy to act — on 1st November 1961, the federal government issued a desegregation order on all interstate buses and trains.

The Civil Rights Movement

These activities are all about how activists fought against Jim Crow Laws during the Civil Rights movement.

Knowledge and Understanding

1) Copy and complete the timeline below by describing the key events in the Civil Rights movement that took place in each year. Give as much detail as possible.

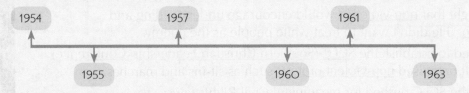

1954   1957   1961

1955   1960   1963

2) Why was it difficult to enforce desegregation in public schools after the Supreme Court's ruling in Brown v Board of Education of Topeka?

3) What was the NAACP? What did it do to challenge racial discrimination in America?

Thinking Historically

1) Copy and complete the table below by explaining the significance of each event for the progress of the Civil Rights movement as a whole.

Event	Significance
a) **Brown v Board of Education**	
b) **The Montgomery Bus Boycott**	
c) **The Greensboro Sit-Ins**	
d) **The Freedom Rides**	

2) Which event in the table above do you think was most significant for the progress of the Civil Rights movement as a whole? Explain your answer.

The beginning of the end for Jim Crow...

It's important to know about the key events in the Civil Rights movement — when and where they happened, what happened, who was involved and what the outcome was.

Martin Luther King and Malcolm X

All Civil Rights leaders, like Martin Luther King and Malcolm X, had a similar aim — justice for African Americans in the USA. However, they didn't always agree on the best method for achieving that aim.

Martin Luther King promoted Non-Violent protest

1) Martin Luther King was a Christian minister. He believed in non-violence and encouraged activists to use non-violent direct action to gain equality.

2) King thought that non-violence would encourage understanding and integration. He didn't want to treat white people as the enemy.

3) King helped to establish the SCLC (Southern Christian Leadership Conference) in 1957. It organised non-violent protests such as sit-ins and marches.

4) King and the SCLC pushed for meaningful Civil Rights laws:

Birmingham

- In April 1963, the SCLC organised marches and sit-ins to try to desegregate Birmingham. The protesters were arrested, including King.

- Police attacked children who joined the marches in May 1963. Images of this led to public outrage. A desegregation agreement was reached, which some white people opposed. Bombers then targeted King, which led some African Americans to riot.

- These events increased sympathy for the Civil Rights movement and persuaded President Kennedy that strong action was needed. In June, he presented a Civil Rights bill to Congress.

March on Washington

- King and the SCLC organised a huge march on Washington DC on 28th August 1963. More than 250,000 people attended.

- During the march, King gave his famous 'I Have a Dream' speech, calling for an end to racism in the USA.

- The march showed that there was massive support for action on Civil Rights, and it received huge media attention. This put pressure on Congress to pass Kennedy's Civil Rights bill.

Other leaders promoted Black Separatism and Violent protest

1) Malcolm X was an influential leader in an African-American organisation called the Nation of Islam. The Nation of Islam encouraged black separatism — the idea that, if black people couldn't achieve freedom, justice and equality in US society, then they should leave and form their own separate nation.

2) Malcolm X criticised the Civil Rights movement — he thought that non-violence was ineffective and would not achieve change. He said that African Americans should use 'any means necessary', even violence, to get equality.

3) Unlike Martin Luther King, Malcolm X saw white people as the enemy — he openly condemned them for their role in oppressing African Americans.

4) Malcolm X encouraged black people to take pride in their African heritage. His preaching helped to raise African-American confidence and self-esteem.

> After he left the Nation of Islam in 1964, Malcolm X moved away from black separatism and began to preach non-violence. He was killed by Nation of Islam members in February 1965.

5) In 1966, the idea of 'Black Power' was popularised by Stokely Carmichael, chairman of the SNCC (Student Nonviolent Coordinating Committee). Under his influence, the SNCC became more radical.

- Carmichael argued that the racism and inequality in US society could only be tackled by strengthening black communities and making them more independent of white society.

- The Black Panther Party, founded in 1966 by Huey Newton and Bobby Seale, embraced 'Black Power'. Its members went on armed patrol, claiming to defend African Americans from police violence.

- The party also tried to strengthen black communities by carrying out education and healthcare programmes. They became extremely popular, especially in deprived inner-city areas.

Martin Luther King and Malcolm X

These activities should give you a better idea of the how the Civil Rights movement progressed in the 1960s.

Knowledge and Understanding

1) Copy and complete the table below by describing the views of Martin Luther King and Malcolm X on the following topics.

   Your answers should focus on Malcolm X's views until 1964.

Topic	Martin Luther King	Malcolm X
a) Use of Violence		
b) Integration		
c) White People		

2) How did Malcolm X's views change after he left the Nation of Islam in 1964?

3) Copy and complete the flowchart below by filling in the missing information about events in Birmingham in 1963.

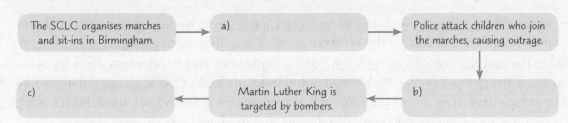

The SCLC organises marches and sit-ins in Birmingham. → a) → Police attack children who join the marches, causing outrage. ↓

c) ← Martin Luther King is targeted by bombers. ← b)

4) Using the following key words, describe the SCLC's March on Washington and its impact.

   28th August 1963   crowd   speech   media attention

5) Give three ways in which the Black Panther Party tried to improve the lives of African Americans.

Thinking Historically

1) Explain how the lives of African Americans were affected by the ideas and actions of each of the following people. Give as much detail as possible.

   a) Martin Luther King   b) Malcolm X   c) Stokely Carmichael

---

EXAM TIP

There were divisions in the Civil Rights movement...

In the exam, you'll lose marks if you don't stay on topic. Highlighting the key words in the question before you answer it will help you to focus on what you've been asked to discuss.

Post-War America

The Civil Rights Acts of 1964 and 1968

The Civil Rights Acts of 1964 and 1968 outlawed segregation and racial discrimination in the USA. This was a huge achievement for the Civil Rights movement, but there was still work to be done to gain full equality.

President Johnson passed the Civil Rights Act in 1964

In June 1963, President Kennedy had presented the Civil Rights bill to Congress (see p.48). However, it is difficult to pass laws in Congress, and Civil Rights was a controversial issue that faced strong resistance from some members of Congress. Therefore, it was unclear how long it would take Kennedy to push the bill through, or whether it was possible at all. Kennedy was assassinated in November 1963 before he could get the bill passed.

1) President Lyndon B. Johnson was Kennedy's successor. Like Kennedy, he was committed to ending segregation. He used the wave of emotion that followed Kennedy's assassination to gain support for the Civil Rights bill, and his skilful negotiation meant that the bill finally became law in June 1964.

2) The eleven sections of the Civil Rights Act:

- Outlawed discrimination in public facilities, such as hotels, restaurants, theatres and parks.
- Encouraged the desegregation of public schools and universities.
- Promoted equal access to job opportunities and banned discrimination in the workplace.
- Strengthened rules against discrimination in voter registration.

The Civil Rights Act had a Lasting Impact on American Society

1) The act forced the federal government to protect minorities from discrimination. Although the government's powers to enforce the act were weak at first, they were gradually strengthened.

2) It led to the introduction of 'affirmative action' — businesses and government agencies actively tried to increase the number of African Americans and other under-represented groups that they employed.

3) Other groups who faced discrimination, such as women (see p.54 and 56), used the act as a blueprint.

4) Although the act outlawed many forms of discrimination, there were shortcomings:

- All of the barriers that prevented African Americans from voting were only officially removed when the Voting Rights Act was passed in 1965.

- The act couldn't immediately end racial discrimination or get rid of racist beliefs. Many African Americans in the North felt that the Civil Rights movement made little difference to their daily lives — they still suffered inequality.

Some African Americans in the North began to believe that change could only be achieved through a more aggressive approach (see p.48). Between 1964 and 1972, there were more than 750 inner-city riots by African Americans. The assassination of Martin Luther King in April 1968 sparked riots in more than 100 cities. This violence and King's murder showed that there were still many problems to overcome.

The 1968 Civil Rights Act addressed Housing

The 1964 act opened the way for more Civil Rights legislation.

1) The 1968 Civil Rights Act, known as the Fair Housing Act, aimed to eliminate racial discrimination in housing.

2) Before 1968, African Americans often found that their attempts to buy or rent homes in certain areas were denied (see p.44). This forced them into overcrowded and poorly built neighbourhoods away from white communities.

3) The act made it illegal to refuse to sell or rent a house to anyone because of their race, colour, religion or nationality.

4) However, powers to enforce the act were limited and people continued to discriminate against African Americans in housing in ways that were less obvious and harder to prove.

Comment and Analysis

Continued discrimination against African Americans showed that, although Civil Rights legislation was a very positive step, real change was unlikely to happen while people continued to hold racist attitudes.

For example, many estate agents continued to steer African Americans away from white neighbourhoods. This didn't encourage integration.

The Civil Rights Acts of 1964 and 1968

Try these activities to understand the impact of the Civil Rights Acts on US society and African Americans.

Knowledge and Understanding

1) Why did Lyndon B. Johnson succeed in passing the 1964 Civil Rights Act?

2) Copy and complete the mind map below by adding
   the changes introduced by the 1964 Civil Rights Act.

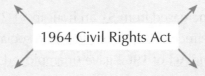

1964 Civil Rights Act

3) Why was the 1968 Civil Rights Act introduced? How did it change the law in America?

4) What were the limitations of the 1968 Civil Rights Act? Give as much detail as possible.

Interpretation

The interpretation below is from an article by David Filvaroff and Raymond Wolfinger, published in 2000. Filvaroff worked as a government official in the Justice Department, and was heavily involved in drafting the 1964 Civil Rights Act. Wolfinger worked as an assistant to a senator who was crucial in passing the Civil Rights Act through Congress.

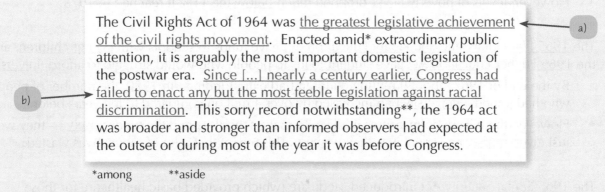

The Civil Rights Act of 1964 was the greatest legislative achievement of the civil rights movement. Enacted amid* extraordinary public attention, it is arguably the most important domestic legislation of the postwar era. Since [...] nearly a century earlier, Congress had failed to enact any but the most feeble legislation against racial discrimination. This sorry record notwithstanding**, the 1964 act was broader and stronger than informed observers had expected at the outset or during most of the year it was before Congress.

a)

b)

*among   **aside

1) For each highlighted phrase, explain whether or not you think it is convincing about the 1964 Civil Rights Act. Use information from page 50 and earlier in the book to help you.

2) Why do you think the interpretation gives a positive view of the 1964 Civil Rights Act? Use the background information about the authors to explain your answer.

The Civil Rights Acts — a sign of progress...

It's important to use examples from your own knowledge to back up your answers in the exam, so make sure you know about the Civil Rights Acts and how the law changed because of them.

The 'Great Society'

The USA still had high levels of inequality after the Second World War. In the 1960s, the Democratic Party, led by Presidents Kennedy and Johnson, brought in reforms to try to wipe out poverty in America.

Kennedy wanted to solve Problems in American Society

1) There were huge economic divisions in American society in the 1950s and 1960s — while many Americans experienced great prosperity, many others were trapped in poverty (see p.38).

2) When Kennedy was elected as President in November 1960, he tried to tackle poverty through a programme of reform called the 'New Frontier'. He passed legislation to improve the lives of the poor:

- The minimum wage was increased from $1 an hour to $1.25 for over 27 million workers.
- Around 4.4 million people received new or increased social security benefits.
- The Manpower and Training Act of 1962 gave unemployed people the opportunity to retrain.

3) However, Congress opposed some of Kennedy's plans to introduce affordable medical care and investment in education — this prevented the reforms from going as far as Kennedy would have liked.

Johnson's 'Great Society' promised to Eradicate Poverty

1) After Kennedy's death in 1963, President Johnson wanted to carry on Kennedy's work. He aimed to make America a fairer and more equal society for everyone.

2) In 1964, Johnson announced a 'war on poverty' with the goal of making the USA a 'Great Society'. As part of his 'Great Society' programme, Johnson introduced legislation to tackle poverty, and to improve education and healthcare:

> Johnson managed to achieve some of the things that Kennedy didn't — he was very skilled at getting reforms through Congress.

Poverty

The 1964 Economic Opportunity Act introduced a Job Corps to give training to young people and help them find jobs. It also gave grants for adult education and gave assistance to needy children.
- 19% of the population were living in poverty in 1964. This had dropped to about 11% by 1973.
- However, levels of poverty never dropped much below the 11% it reached in 1973.

Education

The 1965 Elementary and Secondary Education Act gave funds to schools with poorer children, and the 1965 Higher Education Act gave student loans to people who would struggle to afford university.
- By the end of 1967, about 9 million children had extra funding. In 1970, the number of people who had joined a university had increased by over 4 million compared to ten years before.
- However, there were no measures in place to make schools spend the funds wisely — they were just given money and spent it as they wished. This meant that a lot of money was wasted.

Healthcare

The 1965 Social Security Act introduced Medicare (which provided basic healthcare for those over 65 years old) and Medicaid (which provided basic healthcare for those too poor to afford it).
- Around 19 million people had signed up to Medicare by the end of 1966.
- Medicare payments were made only to hospitals that kept black and white patients together — so it desegregated many hospitals. This was an improvement for Civil Rights as well as healthcare.

3) The 'Great Society' helped to reduce levels of poverty. It was often successful in making it easier for poor people to get a good education and making healthcare more affordable for the poor and the elderly.

4) However, the programme didn't manage to eliminate poverty. This created frustration among the poorest in American society, whose hopes had been raised by Johnson's promises.

5) The programme was also very expensive for the government. In the 1960s, the Vietnam War was costing the US government billions of dollars every year — this took funding away from the 'Great Society'.

6) These limitations played a role in sparking the inner-city riots of the late 1960s and early 1970s (see p.50).

The 'Great Society'

Take a look at the activities below to get to grips with the Democratic Party's attempts to tackle poverty.

Knowledge and Understanding

1) Give three ways in which Kennedy's 'New Frontier' programme improved poor people's lives.

2) Why didn't the 'New Frontier' programme go as far as Kennedy wanted?

3) Make a list of the legislation that was introduced as part of the 'Great Society' programme. For each piece of legislation, explain what changed as a result.

Interpretation

Interpretation 1

Under... the Great Society, there was a dramatic acceleration of governmental efforts to ensure the wellbeing of all citizens; to equalize opportunity for minorities and the disadvantaged; to eliminate, or at least mitigate*, the social, economic, and legal foundations of inequality and deprivation**. Congress moved ahead on a vast range of long-debated social welfare measures and pushed on into uncharted*** seas.

An extract from a journal article by Sar Levitan and Robert Taggart, published in 1976. Levitan was an expert on social and economic policy who worked to create policies to tackle poverty under the 'New Frontier'. Taggart worked as Levitan's research assistant.

*reduce   **poverty   ***unexplored

Interpretation 2

The Great Society programs had poured billions of dollars into supplying a formidable range of social services for the poor; if you could prove that your income was below a certain level you could qualify for any number of free or subsidized* goods or services. I felt that this kind of approach encouraged a feeling of dependence and discouraged the kind of self-reliance that is needed to get people on their feet. I thought that people should have the responsibility for spending carefully and taking care of themselves.

An extract from Richard Nixon's memoirs, published in 1978. Nixon was a Republican President who served after President Johnson. He made changes to the 'Great Society' programme and supported a policy of giving money, rather than services, to the poor.

*partly paid for

1) Which interpretation gives a more positive view of the 'Great Society'? Use details from both interpretations to support your answer.

2) Why do you think these interpretations give different views about the 'Great Society'? Explain your answer, using the background information about each author to help you.

The 'Alright But Not That Great Society'? You decide...

When you're looking at a pair of interpretations, take a couple of minutes to figure out what their main messages are. This will help you to explain how they're different from each other.

Women's Rights

In the 1960s, <u>feminism</u> gained momentum in the USA and began to <u>challenge discrimination</u> against women.

Women were Discouraged from pursuing a Career

1) Traditional <u>gender stereotypes</u> discouraged women from pursuing a career. In the <u>'ideal' American family</u>, women were expected to be <u>housewives</u> and <u>mothers</u> while their husbands worked.

2) In the 1960s, women made up around <u>33-43%</u> of the workforce. They usually worked in <u>low-paid</u> jobs, like cleaning, nursing and teaching. On average, women earned <u>40% less</u> than men.

Women began to challenge Discrimination at Work

1) <u>Eleanor Roosevelt</u> persuaded President Kennedy to create the <u>Presidential Commission on the Status of Women</u> (sometimes called Status Commission 1963) with herself as its head. This was the <u>first time</u> that the federal government had taken the question of <u>women's rights</u> and roles seriously as a <u>political issue</u>.

> The President asked the Commission to <u>investigate inequality</u> between men and women at <u>work</u> and in the USA's <u>taxation</u> and <u>legal systems</u>. The Commission was asked to make <u>recommendations</u> for ways the government could <u>prevent discrimination</u> against women and <u>improve</u> their <u>employment opportunities</u>.

2) The Commission's report, which was published in <u>October 1963</u>, showed that <u>discrimination</u> against women was a <u>serious problem</u> and criticised the <u>gender inequality</u> in American society.

> For example, employers often gave <u>different job titles</u> to men and women who were doing <u>the same job</u>. This enabled them to <u>get around</u> the <u>Equal Pay Act</u> and continue paying men more than women for the same job. The EEOC <u>failed</u> to <u>prevent</u> this practice.

3) In <u>response</u> to the Commission's report, <u>new laws</u> were introduced to give women equality in employment. The <u>1963 Equal Pay Act</u> made it <u>illegal</u> to pay women less than men for the <u>same job</u>. A year later, the <u>1964 Civil Rights Act</u> prohibited discrimination in <u>employment</u> on the basis of <u>sex</u>.

4) However, the new laws weren't enforced properly. The <u>Equal Employment Opportunity Commission</u> (<u>EEOC</u>) was supposed to ensure equality at work, but it focused on <u>racial discrimination</u> and <u>failed</u> to take discrimination against women seriously.

The campaign group NOW was formed in 1966

1) By 1966, activists like <u>Betty Friedan</u> were frustrated at the EEOC's failure to enforce equality for women at work. They founded the <u>National Organisation for Women</u> (<u>NOW</u>) to campaign for women's <u>legal</u>, <u>educational</u> and <u>professional equality</u>.

> In 1963, Betty Friedan published '<u>The Feminine Mystique</u>', based on her research among America's suburban housewives. The book described women's <u>dissatisfaction</u> with the roles of <u>housewife</u> and <u>mother</u>. She argued that women were just as <u>capable</u> of pursuing a <u>career</u> as men, and that confining women to traditionally feminine roles <u>wasted</u> their <u>talents and potential</u>. 'The Feminine Mystique' was <u>highly influential</u> and played an <u>important role</u> in the development of <u>feminism</u> in the USA in the 1960s.

2) NOW took the step of drafting their own <u>Bill of Rights</u> in 1968. The bill demanded that <u>gender equality</u> was written into the Constitution. They also wanted access to <u>equal employment rights</u> and <u>job opportunities</u>, paid <u>maternity leave</u>, access to <u>child care</u> and the right to have an <u>abortion</u>.

3) NOW used similar tactics to the African-American Civil Rights movement. They <u>petitioned</u> the EEOC, <u>demonstrated</u> at EEOC offices, <u>disrupted</u> Senate hearings, launched <u>legal challenges</u> to sex discrimination, and organised <u>marches</u> and <u>boycotts</u> of companies that discriminated against women.

Women's rights campaigners marching in Washington DC as part of the Women's Strike for Equality.

4) On <u>26th August 1970</u>, NOW supported the <u>Women's Strike for Equality</u>, with demonstrations in more than 90 US towns and cities. Around <u>20,000</u> people participated in a march in <u>New York</u>.

Women's Rights

Test your knowledge on the campaign for gender equality in 1960s America by taking a look at this page.

Knowledge and Understanding

1) Copy and complete the table below, explaining how each development challenged gender discrimination in America.

Development	How it challenged gender discrimination
a) Presidential Commission on the Status of Women	
b) Equal Pay Act (1963)	
c) Civil Rights Act (1964)	

2) What was 'NOW'? Why was it founded?

3) Copy and complete the mind map below by giving the demands that NOW made in their 1968 Bill of Rights.

Demands in NOW's 1968 Bill of Rights

4) Give five examples of tactics used by NOW to campaign for women's rights.

Thinking Historically

1) Explain why each of the following was a problem for women in the 1960s. Give as much detail as possible.

a) The widespread nature of gender stereotypes.

b) The treatment of women at work.

c) The government's failure to enforce new legislation.

Women faced discrimination at home and in the workplace...

Make sure you know what life was like for women before feminism gained momentum in America. It'll help you to write about how the fight against inequality changed their lives.

Women's Rights

The women's movement <u>achieved</u> a lot for women — including the right to <u>equal pay</u> and <u>equal educational opportunities</u>. However, <u>strong opposition</u> meant feminists <u>weren't</u> able to achieve all their goals.

Activists improved Equality in Employment and Education

1) Pressure from NOW and other women's rights groups forced the <u>EEOC</u> to take discrimination <u>seriously</u>. From the late 1960s, it <u>enforced</u> the laws that were meant to improve <u>gender equality</u> in work (see p.54).

2) In <u>1968</u>, the EEOC <u>outlawed</u> job advertisements that asked for <u>men only</u>. This meant that women could apply for <u>higher paid</u> jobs from which they had previously been <u>excluded</u>.

3) In <u>1971</u>, the <u>Supreme Court</u> ruled in the case <u>Reed v Reed</u> that laws discriminating against women were <u>unconstitutional</u>. This was the <u>first time</u> that the Supreme Court had used the <u>14th Amendment</u>, which guarantees equal protection under the law to all citizens, to protect <u>women's rights</u>. The Supreme Court also issued rulings against sex discrimination in <u>employment</u> in 1971 and 1973.

> <u>Reed v Reed</u> was a case that challenged a law in Idaho which stated that <u>men</u> should have <u>priority</u> if two people claimed to be equally entitled to a relative's inheritance. The <u>Supreme Court</u> ruled that this was discrimination under the <u>14th Amendment</u>.

4) The <u>Educational Amendments Act</u> (1972) forced public <u>educational establishments</u> to provide equal facilities and opportunities for both sexes. This was an extension of the <u>1964 Civil Rights Act</u>, which had outlawed sex discrimination at <u>work</u>, but not in <u>public education</u>.

> The Educational Amendments Act also extended the <u>1963 Equal Pay Act</u>. The Act had banned <u>gender discrimination</u> in pay for a lot of jobs, but it was now <u>expanded</u> to include <u>executive</u>, <u>administrative</u> and <u>professional</u> jobs as well.

There was Strong Opposition to some feminist campaigns

Much like the Civil Rights movement, feminist campaigns faced determined <u>resistance</u>.

Abortion

- Feminists believed that women had the <u>right</u> to choose <u>abortion</u>. The Supreme Court ruled in the case <u>Roe v Wade</u> (1973) that state laws banning abortion were <u>unconstitutional</u>. Women now had <u>power</u> over their own bodies and the right to <u>choose</u> whether they wanted an abortion or not.
- But in response to pressure from religious groups, Congress passed the <u>Hyde Amendment</u> in <u>1976</u>. This stopped <u>Medicaid</u> (the medical assistance programme for the poor) from <u>funding</u> abortions.
- Without government funding, abortion became <u>too expensive</u> for many women on <u>low incomes</u>.

Equal Rights Amendment

- NOW campaigned for the <u>Equal Rights Amendment</u> (<u>ERA</u>), a constitutional amendment to <u>guarantee equal rights</u> for women. It was passed by <u>Congress</u> in <u>1972</u>, and most of the public supported it. To become law, the bill needed to be <u>ratified</u> (approved) by <u>38</u> of the <u>50 states</u>.
- However, the bill faced <u>opposition</u> from women, such as Phyllis Schlafly, who wanted a return to <u>traditional femininity</u>. Schlafly, a conservative activist, didn't believe in women having <u>equality</u> with men — she wanted women to be <u>protected</u> and <u>provided for</u> in their role as <u>wife</u> and <u>mother</u>.
- Schlafly argued that the amendment would lead to more <u>abortions</u>, women being <u>drafted</u> into the Army and <u>fighting</u> on the front line, and a wider acceptance of <u>homosexuality</u>. These arguments gained her <u>support</u> from <u>conservative people</u> and <u>religious groups</u> in America.
- Schlafly founded the '<u>STOP ERA</u>' campaign. She staged rallies to <u>pressure</u> states into <u>rejecting</u> the ERA, with her followers <u>baking pies</u> for politicians to show their value as <u>homemakers</u>.
- As a result of Schlafly's campaign, ratification <u>slowed</u> and some states that had already ratified the ERA <u>withdrew</u> their support. In the end, only <u>35</u> of the required <u>38</u> states ratified the ERA, which meant that it <u>didn't</u> become <u>law</u>.

> **Comment and Analysis**
>
> This was a <u>serious blow</u> to <u>feminists</u> and the fight for <u>gender equality</u>. Opposition to the ERA and other feminist campaigns shows that some people in America were still <u>not convinced</u> about giving women <u>more rights</u>.

Women's Rights

This page will help you to understand what the women's rights campaign achieved in the 1960s and 1970s.

Knowledge and Understanding

1) How did the Educational Amendments Act extend each of the following acts?

    a) 1963 Equal Pay Act   b) 1964 Civil Rights Act

2) What was the Hyde Amendment? Why was it passed?

3) What was the ERA? Why did some women oppose it?

4) Why didn't the ERA become law, even though it was passed by Congress in 1972?

Thinking Historically

1) Copy and complete the diagram below by giving the outcome of each Supreme Court case and explaining its significance for women's rights.

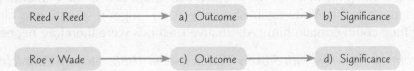

Reed v Reed → a) Outcome → b) Significance

Roe v Wade → c) Outcome → d) Significance

2) Do you think political campaigns or legal rulings were more important in reducing gender inequality in the 1960s and 1970s? Use the table to help you structure each paragraph of an essay that answers the question above.

Point	Evidence	Why evidence supports point?
Campaigns in the 1960s and 1970s put pressure on the government to pass new laws that gave more rights to women.	NOW campaigned for access to equal employment rights and job opportunities. In 1968, the EEOC outlawed men-only job advertisements.	One of the reasons why the EEOC started to take gender discrimination seriously was the pressure created by NOW. This suggests that political campaigns were very important in reducing gender inequality.

Add three rows to the table to create three more paragraphs.

You can use evidence from pages 54 and 56 to back up your points.

NOW's a good time for you to start revising women's rights...

Before answering the 12-mark question in the exam, write out a quick plan. This will help you to structure your argument and make sure you don't forget to mention any important points.

Worked Exam-Style Questions

The sample answers on the next few pages will help you prepare for the first five questions of the exam.

Interpretation 1

Physically, nonviolence is no problem. If someone spits on you, you wipe it off. It's not going to kill you... But then, a person with a good heart and is willing and committed gets the hell beat out of him with seemingly no results. That happened a lot in the '60s, and you'd ask yourself, "Why am I doing this?" The answer is: it works in the long run. Others see the bandages and get stirred up and want to do something about it. What do we want them to do, simply raise some money and go to court? No, we want them to join us, and many of them did.

An extract from an interview with Bernard Lafayette in 2007. Lafayette was involved in the creation of the SNCC and took part in several forms of non-violent protest, including sit-ins and Freedom Rides. He was beaten and arrested on multiple occasions. He eventually left the SNCC to join the SCLC after Martin Luther King offered him a prominent position there.

Interpretation 2

No one who truly understands the struggle can in any way fault King... Of course his political errors are to be understood. But I mean in terms of his commitment, in terms of his total love. In terms of his total dedication to the struggle, one can find no shortcomings here. But... unfortunately the system had learned how to contain non violent demonstrations. Having learned how to contain them, it was not necessary for them to respond to them. Thus, King was not failing as much as the White establishment was no longer responding to him, having now thought that they could contain him. Alternative methods were therefore necessary.

An extract from an interview with Stokely Carmichael in 1988. Stokely Carmichael was heavily involved in the SNCC and originally supported non-violence. However, he became frustrated with this approach and took the SNCC in a more militant direction after becoming its chairman.

Look at Interpretation 1 and Interpretation 2. In what ways do the authors' views differ about the effectiveness of non-violence? Use both interpretations to explain your answer. [4 marks]

> Identify the **main opinion** given in each interpretation.

> Use **evidence** from the interpretations to **back up** your points.

> This answer highlights **more than one** feature of the interpretation.

Interpretation 1 argues that non-violence was an effective way of protesting during the Civil Rights movement. According to Lafayette, when non-violent protesters became victims of violence, they were achieving their aims because other people saw their injuries and were encouraged to 'do something about it'. Therefore, Lafayette claims that non-violence 'works in the long run' by drawing attention to an issue or problem.

In contrast, Interpretation 2 suggests that non-violent demonstrations became ineffective because 'the system had learned how to contain' them. Carmichael claims that protesters such as Martin Luther King, who only used non-violent methods, stopped making progress because 'the White establishment' was able to ignore their protests. Carmichael argues that other methods of protest were necessary instead.

Worked Exam-Style Questions

Explain why the authors of Interpretation 1 and Interpretation 2 might have different views about the effectiveness of non-violence. Use both interpretations and your own knowledge in your answer.   [4 marks]

The first sentence directly addresses the question.

You could write about each author's beliefs and how this might have affected their interpretation.

Think about the authors' different experiences.

The two authors might have different views because they had different political beliefs. Lafayette seems to have been committed to non-violence. He participated in lots of non-violent protests and was involved with the SCLC, which organised non-violent protests like sit-ins and marches. Therefore, he defends the effectiveness of non-violence in Interpretation 1. On the other hand, Carmichael's role in making the SNCC more militant shows that he believed in a more radical approach to protesting. This means that Interpretation 2 questions the effectiveness of non-violence and argues for other forms of protest instead.

The interpretations might also be different because the two authors had different ideas about the aim of protesting. As a member of the SCLC, Lafayette probably supported its aim of achieving equality between white people and African Americans by encouraging integration. Given that protests like the Montgomery Bus Boycott and Greensboro Sit-Ins successfully integrated many public facilities in the South, Lafayette is likely to view non-violent protest as effective. In contrast, Carmichael popularised the idea of 'Black Power', which involved strengthening black communities to make them more independent of white communities. Protests like the ones in Montgomery and Greensboro did not necessarily strengthen black communities in the way Carmichael wanted, so he is less likely to view these methods as effective.

Worked Exam-Style Questions

Do you think Interpretation 1 or Interpretation 2 is more convincing about the effectiveness of non-violence? Use both interpretations and your own knowledge to explain your answer.   [8 marks]

In Interpretation I, Lafayette argues that non-violence was effective because it encouraged 'many' protesters to join the Civil Rights movement. This is convincing because organisations like the SCLC succeeded in gathering large crowds to support them. For example, the SCLC organised a march on Washington DC on 28th August 1963 that was attended by over 250,000 people. The march showed that there was massive support for the Civil Rights movement and put pressure on Congress to pass Kennedy's Civil Rights bill.

Lafayette's claim that non-violence 'works in the long run' is partially convincing because many forms of non-violent protest were eventually successful. For example, the 1955 Montgomery Bus Boycott led to a Supreme Court ruling that Alabama's bus segregation laws were unconstitutional, while the 1960 Greensboro Sit-Ins led to the desegregation of a department store lunch counter. The marches and sit-ins to desegregate Birmingham in April and May 1963 were not only successful in achieving their aim, but also helped to convince Kennedy to present his Civil Rights bill to Congress.

Although non-violent protests often achieved legal changes, Carmichael's claim in Interpretation 2 that they were ineffective because 'the system had learned how to contain' them is partially convincing. This is because, despite King's campaign for meaningful Civil Rights laws, changes to the law that were introduced in response to non-violent protests often had a limited impact. People continued to hold racist beliefs, and they continued to discriminate against African Americans. For example, the 1968 Civil Rights Act made it illegal to refuse to sell or rent a house to someone because of their race, but many estate agents got around this law by steering African Americans away from white neighbourhoods. The limited impact of legal changes like the 1968 Civil Rights Act meant that many African Americans, especially those in the North, thought that the Civil Rights movement had made little difference to their lives. This supports Carmichael's claim about the limitations of non-violent protest, as well as making Lafayette's argument that non-violence 'works in the long run' less convincing.

Overall, both interpretations are only partially convincing because they both give a one-sided view of the effectiveness of non-violence. Lafayette considers the achievements of non-violent protest without discussing its limitations, while Carmichael only focuses on the limitations of non-violence without acknowledging the important progress that non-violent protests made.

Analyse the main arguments in each interpretation.

Give a clear opinion about how convincing you find each interpretation.

Including specific details like dates and statistics shows good knowledge of the topic.

This shows that you've considered both sides of the argument.

Use your own knowledge to help you decide whether each interpretation is convincing or not.

Make a clear judgement on how convincing the interpretations are at the end of your answer.

Worked Exam-Style Questions

Describe two difficulties that the women's rights campaign faced in the 1960s and 1970s.   [4 marks]

Make sure you clearly identify two <u>separate</u> difficulties.

Try to address the question <u>directly</u> in the <u>first sentence</u>.

One difficulty that the women's rights campaign faced in the 1960s and 1970s was that laws which were introduced to give women greater equality weren't always enforced. The 1963 Equal Pay Act was meant to make it illegal to pay women less than men for the same job, and the 1964 Civil Rights Act banned discrimination in employment on the basis of sex. However, the EEOC didn't enforce these laws properly because it focused on racial discrimination and failed to take gender discrimination seriously. Employers were therefore able to get around these laws, and discrimination against women at work continued.

Another difficulty that the women's rights campaign faced was opposition from conservative people. For example, in 1972, Congress passed the Equal Rights Amendment to guarantee equal rights for women. However, the conservative activist Phyllis Schlafly campaigned against the amendment. She gained support from other conservatives and religious groups, and the amendment wasn't ratified by enough states for it to become law. This shows that a lot of people still weren't convinced about giving equal rights to women.

Show you understand <u>why</u> each factor was <u>problematic</u>.

62

Worked Exam-Style Questions

Explain how people's lives were affected by President Kennedy and President Johnson's attempts to tackle poverty.   [8 marks]

Briefly explain your argument in the first sentence.Briefly <u>explain</u> your argument in the first sentence.

Kennedy and Johnson's attempts to tackle poverty had a major impact on the lives of Americans, but different groups were affected in different ways and the impact of their policies changed over time. Under Kennedy's 'New Frontier' programme, introduced in 1960, over 27 million workers benefited from an increase in the minimum wage from $1 to $1.25 an hour, while around 4.4 million Americans received new or increased social security benefits. However, opposition from Congress meant that the reforms didn't go as far as Kennedy wanted, and 19% of America was still living in poverty by 1964. During Johnson's presidency, laws like the 1964 Economic Opportunity Act helped to pull more people out of poverty by giving them employment and educational opportunities. As a result, the percentage of people living in poverty had dropped to about 11% in 1973.

Explain how <u>different groups</u> were affected in <u>different ways</u>.

Children and young people particularly benefited from the development of Johnson's 'Great Society' after 1964. The 1964 Economic Opportunity Act gave assistance to needy children and introduced a Job Corps to give training to young people and to help them to find jobs. Children also benefited from the 1964 Elementary and Secondary Education Act, which gave funding to schools with poorer children. These policies affected the lives of a huge number of children and young people. By the end of 1967, around 9 million children had received extra funding. However, the policies had some limitations. For example, there were no measures in place to control how the money from the Elementary and Secondary Education Act was spent, so a lot of it was wasted.

This <u>links back</u> to the question by explaining <u>how</u> Johnson's policies affected people's lives.

Johnson's 'Great Society' also improved access to healthcare for poorer people and the elderly. The 1965 Social Security Act meant that poorer people were given access to basic healthcare under the Medicaid scheme, while people over 65 years old received basic healthcare under the Medicare scheme.

Use <u>detailed examples</u> to <u>support</u> your points.

Around 19 million people had signed up for Medicare by the end of 1966, demonstrating its widespread impact on the lives of elderly people in America.

However, Kennedy and Johnson's attempts to tackle poverty failed to eliminate it completely, which led to frustration among the poorest in society. People's hopes had been raised by Kennedy and Johnson's promises, but factors like the expensive Vietnam War took funding away from the 'war on poverty' and limited its impact. The frustration caused by this played a role in the inner-city riots of the late 1960s and the early 1970s.

Post-War America

Exam-Style Questions

Here are some exam-style questions to put what you've learned throughout the whole section to the test.

Exam-Style Questions

1) Describe two difficulties that African Americans in the South faced as a result of Jim Crow Laws.   [4 marks]

2) Explain how the lives of African Americans were affected by the Civil Rights Acts of 1964 and 1968.   [8 marks]

3) Look at the bullet points below. Which one was the more important consequence of America's post-war prosperity?

   - social changes
   - cultural changes

   Explain your answer, referring to both bullet points.   [12 marks]

Answers

Marking the Activities

We've included sample answers for all the activities. When you're marking your work, remember that our answers are just a guide — some of the activities ask you to give your own opinion, so there is no 'correct answer'.

Marking the Exam-Style Questions

For each exam-style question, we've covered some key points that your answer could include. Our answers are just examples though — answers very different to ours could also get top marks.

Most exam questions in history are level marked. This means the examiner puts your answer into one of several levels. Then they award marks based on how well your answer matches the description for that level.

To reach a higher level, you'll need to give a 'more sophisticated' answer. Exactly what 'sophisticated' means will depend on the type of question, but, generally speaking, a more sophisticated answer could include more detail, more background knowledge or make a more complex judgement.

Start by choosing which level your answer falls into. A good way to do this is to start at 'Level 1' and go up to the next level each time your answer meets all the conditions of a level. Next, choose a mark. The mark you choose will depend on whether you think you've met all of, most of, or some of the conditions in that level.

American People and the 'Boom'

Page 5 — The 'Boom' and its Impact
Thinking Historically
1 a) People could pay for expensive goods in instalments, rather than paying up front. This meant that people could more easily afford luxury goods such as hoovers, washing machines and cars.
   b) It was easy for people to take out a loan or make an agreement to take an item and pay for it later. This meant that people were able to buy expensive goods that they wouldn't otherwise have been able to afford, improving their standard of living.
   c) Advertising encouraged people to spend more by persuading them to buy goods. The use of newspapers, magazines and posters, as well as technologies such as film and radio, meant that more people were reached and influenced by advertising.
   d) Companies were able to produce goods in large quantities thanks to mass production. It also allowed them to produce these goods more cheaply. Therefore, companies could sell mass-produced goods at lower prices, meaning that more people could afford to buy them.
   e) The stock market boom gave some people the chance to become rich by buying shares using credit, waiting for their value to go up, then selling them for profit. These people were called speculators.

Interpretation
1 a) The motor industry stimulated the steel, glass, rubber and petrol industries. The rise in car ownership also created a demand for good roads and roadside services. This meant that the construction industry benefited from building petrol stations, motels and roadside restaurants. Finally, the fact that more people owned cars meant that they could live away from the workplace and drive to work, which boosted house-building as more houses were built in the suburbs.
   b) Millions of people owned cars by the end of the 1920s. Ford's use of assembly lines meant that cars were made quickly, cheaply and in large quantities, so there were lots of cars available to buy, and people could afford to buy them more easily. As a result, many more people were buying cars and using them on the roads.
2 Chase claims that the motor car was the most important factor in creating prosperity in the 1920s. He suggests that the motor car was good because it provided other businesses with a boost and made the country look prosperous. However, Chase also suggests that the motor car wasn't as good for everyone in America as it seemed. He says that the motor car only gave America an 'appearance' of prosperity.

Page 7 — The 'Boom' and its Impact
Knowledge and Understanding
1 It means that the Republican Party thought that the government should not try to control the economy.
2 The term 'rugged individualism' refers to the idea adopted by the Republican Party that Americans should look after themselves instead of relying on the government for help.
3 • Farmers faced the problem of overproduction. There had been a lot of demand in Europe for food from US farms during the First World War. However, farms continued to produce large quantities of food after the war ended. This overproduction meant that food prices fell dramatically. Many farms ran at a loss.
   • Debt was also a problem. Some farmers had taken out loans to expand their farms during the First World War. However, their debts increased when they failed to repay these loans, and some had to sell their farms.
   • Demand for cotton decreased because the textile industry started using man-made synthetic fibres instead. Many southern farmers grew a lot of cotton, so they were particularly badly affected.
   • Farmers who were struggling didn't receive enough help from the government. The McNary-Haugen Bill, which involved the government buying extra supplies of farm products to stop farmers from losing money, was proposed several times. However, President Coolidge vetoed it twice.
   • Many African-American sharecroppers lived in extreme poverty and suffered discrimination due to segregation.

Thinking Historically
1 a) The government took a laissez-faire approach to the economy, which meant that few restrictions were placed on banks, businesses and the stock market. This gave businesses the chance to be successful, helping them to make money and become prosperous.
   b) The government reduced income tax and made sure that other taxes were low. This increased prosperity because it meant that people had more money to spend. The fact that people could spend this money on products from US businesses meant that businesses benefited too.
   c) The Fordney-McCumber Tariff in 1922 made it more expensive for foreign producers to import goods into America. This forced foreign producers to raise their prices to cover the extra cost of the tariff, which meant that American goods were always cheaper than foreign goods. As a result, consumers were more likely to buy American goods, which helped US businesses to prosper.

Answers

2 a) The development of new mining technologies led to coal workers losing their jobs. Those who kept their jobs were paid less. This meant that some people suffered from unemployment and poverty during the 'boom'.

   b) The existence of monopolies meant that there was no competition for customers or workers between companies in some industries, because these industries were controlled by one company or group. This allowed companies to keep prices high and wages low, adding to the poverty that some people were experiencing.

   c) Millions of people migrated from rural areas to urban areas to find work. This meant that there was more competition for the same jobs and housing in towns and cities, which made it difficult for people to find them.

Page 9 — Social and Cultural Developments
Knowledge and Understanding
1
   • Tickets were cheap, which meant that people were more likely to be able to afford to go to the cinema.
   • The introduction of 'talkies' meant that some films started to feature audio instead of being silent. This attracted even more people to the cinema.
   • People enjoyed going to watch movie stars such as Gloria Swanson, Rudolph Valentino and Clara Bow. Clara Bow, for example, was an icon of the decade, with people trying to copy her style and behaviour.

2 Jazz is a genre of music that developed from the music of black communities in the southern states. It became very popular in 1920s America. Some people disapproved of it because its fast-paced rhythm led to daring and suggestive dancing, which was considered immoral.

3 A 'flapper' was a young woman who abandoned the traditional values of her mother's generation. Flappers wore loose dresses and stopped wearing corsets, wore make-up and had short hair. Many flappers smoked, drank alcohol and drove cars.

4
   • Women were still expected to raise children, do housework and stick to traditional values.
   • Many women couldn't afford to live the flapper lifestyle.
   • Some religious women disapproved of flapper behaviour.

Interpretation
1 a) This suggests that women were starting to gain a lot more freedom in the 1920s.

   b) This suggests that the main reason most younger women didn't take part in politics was that they weren't interested in it.

   c) This suggests that gaining the right to vote confirmed that women were equal to men.

2 You can answer either way, as long as you explain your answers. For example:

   a) This is convincing because more women were starting to work and gain access to their own income, with around a quarter of women in employment by 1930. This meant that these women had the money and freedom to live more independently.

   b) This isn't convincing because a lot of women were poor and had to concentrate on working and supporting their families rather than taking part in politics. Many African-American women found it particularly difficult to take part in politics because they often couldn't vote due to racism and prejudice. Many younger women might therefore have been interested in politics, but might not have taken part for other reasons.

   c) This isn't convincing because, although women worked in greater numbers and gained the right to vote, most of them were still expected to raise children, do housework and stick to Victorian morals. This suggests that they weren't equal to men in the 1920s, despite making some progress.

Page 11 — Intolerance and Prejudice
Knowledge and Understanding
1 Before 1890, the majority of immigrants to America came from northern European countries like Britain and Germany.

2 From 1890 onwards, there was a huge increase in the number of immigrants moving to America from southern and eastern European countries such as Italy, Russia and Poland. Many of these 'new' immigrants were unskilled workers with little education, and they were often Catholics or Jews. In contrast, the majority of immigrants to America before 1890 had been well-educated, skilled workers, and they were usually Protestants. They were known as WASPs (white, Anglo-Saxon Protestants).

3 a) Many 'new' immigrants worked for low pay, so Americans worried that cheap immigrant labour would create competition for jobs and cause wages to fall.

   b) There were fears that some 'new' immigrants were communists who would undermine the American way of life. These fears were especially strong during the Red Scare.

   c) Some 'new' immigrants held different religious beliefs to Americans. Most Americans were Protestants, but 'new' immigrants were often Catholics or Jews.

   d) Many Americans blamed immigrants for social problems such as crime, alcoholism and the spread of disease.

4 A lot of 'new' immigrants to America lived in separate communities and spoke their own languages, which meant that they didn't integrate into US society. This created tension with some Americans. Many 'new' immigrants were treated with distrust and suspicion, because people feared that immigration would change America's society and identity. These 'new' immigrants were also exploited at work, working long hours for very little pay. This meant that they could often only afford to live in cramped and dirty housing in the poorest parts of towns and cities.

5 a) • 1917
       • It made it harder for poorly-educated immigrants to gain entry into America because they had to pass the tests to get into the country.

   b) • 1921
       • It introduced quotas to limit the number of immigrants from certain countries. It particularly restricted immigration from southern and eastern Europe.

   c) • 1924
       • It made it harder for certain races such as Africans, Arabs, and southern and eastern Europeans to get into America.

Thinking Historically
1 African Americans in the South faced oppression due to segregation, which forced them to use separate facilities to white people. However, segregation wasn't enforced by law in the North, so African Americans who moved from the South to the North between 1916 and 1929 no longer had to live with official segregation.

2 African Americans in the South often lived in poverty due to discrimination in jobs and housing. This stayed the same for African Americans who moved from the South to the North between 1916 and 1929, as many firms in the North refused to hire them, and any work that they could find was often unskilled and badly paid. They continued to face discrimination in housing too, as African Americans in the North were charged high rents to live in run-down and overcrowded ghettos.

Page 13 — Intolerance and Prejudice
Knowledge and Understanding
1 a) Communists believe that wealth should be shared more equally and that government control over the economy can help to achieve this.

Answers

b) Anarchists believe that laws and government are unnecessary.

2 It means that anyone is free to make a profit from their work, and that wealth isn't shared equally.

3 a) Americans worried that their way of life was under threat from those who disagreed with capitalism, like anarchists and communists. They feared that foreign anarchists and communists might come America and try to change their society.

b) In 1919, workers in Seattle went on strike to demand fair wages. Many Americans were worried that these workers wanted to start a communist revolution like the one in Russia in 1917.

c) Later in 1919, supporters of an Italian anarchist called Luigi Galleani carried out bombings against important figures such as politicians.

d) After the 1919 bombings, the government arrested suspected communists and anarchists in a series of operations called the Palmer Raids. Most of those arrested were immigrants and hundreds of them were deported, even if they'd done nothing wrong. Many of the arrests were illegal because they were made without warrants.

4 Sacco and Vanzetti were anarchists who had moved to America from Italy. Prejudice affected the outcome of their trial because their political views and immigrant status might have been what led the judge to ignore 107 witness statements saying that the two men were elsewhere at the time of the crime, and to refuse them a second trial after another criminal confessed to the crime. They were executed despite a lack of clear-cut evidence.

5 The Ku Klux Klan was a white supremacist organisation based in the southern states that wanted to keep America white and Protestant. African Americans were their main targets, but they also targeted 'new' immigrants, who were often Catholics or Jews.

6 a) The KKK gained popularity in the North in the 1920s because they appealed to WASPS who felt threatened by rising levels of 'new' immigration and by African Americans moving to urban areas.

b) The KKK lost support and political power in 1925 when the Indiana KKK leader, D.C. Stephenson, was convicted of raping and murdering a white woman.

Thinking Historically

1 a) • Many 'new' immigrants faced distrust and suspicion from Americans who feared that immigration would change America's society and identity.
   • Immigrants faced hostility from the Ku Klux Klan, who wanted to keep America a Protestant country. This is because 'new' immigrants were often Catholics or Jews.
   • Many 'new' immigrants were denied entry to America. In response to fears over immigration, the government restricted who could enter the country using literacy tests, the 1921 Emergency Quota Act and the 1924 Johnson-Reed Act.

b) • African Americans in the South faced oppression due to segregation, which forced them to use separate facilities to white people.
   • African Americans across America faced prejudice and discrimination, which made it difficult for them to find jobs and housing.
   • African Americans were often victims of violent crimes committed by the Ku Klux Klan. They were kidnapped, tarred and feathered or even lynched by members of the Ku Klux Klan.

c) • Many suspected communists and anarchists were arrested and deported during the Palmer Raids, even if they'd done nothing wrong.

• People with radical views were treated unfairly by the justice system. It's thought that one of the reasons why Sacco and Vanzetti were wrongly convicted of murder and robbery was that they were anarchists.

Page 15 — Prohibition and Organised Crime
Knowledge and Understanding

1 • 1913 — Temperance groups start campaigning for Prohibition to become law in America.
   • 1919 — The 18th Amendment is approved, banning the production, distribution and sale of alcohol in America.
   • 1920 — Prohibition comes into action in America.
   • 1932 — Roosevelt promises to end Prohibition as part of his presidential campaign.
   • 1933 — The 18th Amendment is withdrawn, meaning that Prohibition is over.

2 • Temperance Groups — They believed that alcohol caused violence, immorality and the breakdown of family life.
   • Middle-Class Americans — They blamed alcohol for immoral behaviour among 'new' immigrants and the working class.
   • Rural Americans — They associated alcohol with high crime rates and violence in rapidly growing US cities.
   • Employers — They thought that alcohol made workers unreliable.
   • Women's Groups — They thought that Prohibition would reduce domestic violence.

3 a) Moonshiners were people who made their own liquor.
   b) Rum-runners were people who smuggled alcohol into America.
   c) Bootleggers were people who took alcohol that was meant to be used in industry and made it drinkable.
   d) Speakeasies were illegal drinking clubs that appeared after Prohibition was introduced.

4 During Prohibition, Al Capone made money from the illegal distribution of alcohol. He did this by gaining control of Chicago's speakeasies after targeting and killing members of rival gangs. As well as earning a lot of money, Al Capone also became an influential figure in US society.

Thinking Historically

1 a) Prohibition led to a fall in crimes linked to alcohol and drunkenness, but a rise in organised crime. Gangs in cities all over America started to fight for control over the illegal distribution of alcohol, which led to extreme violence and even murders. Some judges and policemen accepted bribes from gangsters in return for overlooking their illegal behaviour.

b) Prohibition had negative consequences for the economy, which could have been boosted by taxes on alcohol and jobs in alcohol production.

c) Drinking went down under Prohibition, which might have had positive consequences for people's health. However, people didn't stop drinking altogether, and the illegal alcohol that some people did drink was poor quality. This alcohol caused a lot of deaths.

d) Prohibition added to inequality in America, because poor people couldn't afford to buy illegal alcohol like rich people. This caused resentment among poor people.

2 You can choose any opinion, as long as you explain your answer. For example:
Overall, the consequences of Prohibition were negative for America. Although Prohibition had some positive consequences, such as a fall in drinking and in crimes related to alcohol and drunkenness, these were usually accompanied by negative consequences. For example, organised crime rose at the same time as crimes related to alcohol and drunkenness fell, and this was probably more of a problem due to the extreme violence it caused.

Answers

Pages 16-17 — Exam-Style Questions

1 This question is level marked. How to grade your answer:

Level 1 1-2 marks	The answer gives differences which are supported by some analysis of one or both interpretations.
Level 2 3-4 marks	The answer explains differences which are well supported by analysis of both interpretations.

Here are some points your answer may include:
- Interpretation 1 claims that Prohibition was a success as it caused the disappearance of saloons and gave people more time and money to spend on things other than drinking. Von Luckner argues that instead of spending 'half his wages' in a saloon, a worker could now 'buy his own car' and 'ride off for a weekend or a few days' with his family. In contrast, Interpretation 2 claims that Prohibition was a failure as people continued to drink even though saloons disappeared. Sabin argues that people got around the law by going to a 'speak-easy' or making their own alcohol and 'drinking it furtively'.
- Interpretation 1 suggests that crime went down as a result of Prohibition. Von Luckner claims that the number of 'crimes and misdemeanors' linked to drunkenness 'declined'. In contrast, Interpretation 2 suggests that Prohibition led hundreds of thousands of Americans to commit crime. Sabin claims that a lot of otherwise 'respected citizens' broke the law by buying alcohol.

2 This question is level marked. How to grade your answer:

Level 1 1-2 marks	The answer gives appropriate reasons why the interpretations are different. The reasons are based on a simple analysis of the interpretations' provenance.
Level 2 3-4 marks	The answer gives appropriate reasons why the interpretations are different. The reasons are well supported by knowledge of the period and a detailed analysis of the interpretations' provenance.

Here are some points your answer may include:
- The authors might have different views because they had different perspectives on Prohibition. Felix von Luckner was a high-profile, foreign visitor to America in the late 1920s. He spent his time making speeches and meeting important figures, so is unlikely to have come across the problems that Prohibition caused. This makes him more likely to present Prohibition positively. On the other hand, Pauline Sabin was a Republican Party official who opposed Prohibition from the mid-1920s onwards. As a result, she was almost certainly more aware of the issues that Prohibition caused, meaning that she is more likely to present it negatively.
- The authors might have different views because they were writing for different purposes. Von Luckner was writing an account of his time in America, and is unlikely to criticise the country that welcomed him as a high-profile visitor. In contrast, Sabin was writing an article for a magazine at a time when she was starting to become more outspoken in her opposition to Prohibition. This means that she is likely to use the article to criticise Prohibition.

3 This question is level marked. How to grade your answer:

Level 1 1-2 marks	The answer shows support for one or both interpretations. It is based on a simple analysis of the interpretations and basic knowledge of the topic.
Level 2 3-4 marks	The answer evaluates the credibility of one interpretation. It is supported by a more detailed analysis of the interpretations and some relevant knowledge of the topic.
Level 3 5-6 marks	The answer evaluates the credibility of both interpretations and gives a judgement about which one is more convincing. It is supported by a detailed analysis of the interpretations and a good level of relevant knowledge of the topic.
Level 4 7-8 marks	The answer evaluates the credibility of both interpretations and comes to a clear judgement about which one is more convincing. It is supported by a strong analysis of the interpretations and a wide range of relevant knowledge of the topic.

Here are some points your answer may include:
- Interpretation 1 claims that Prohibition was 'successful' because saloons 'disappeared', which stopped people from drinking. This is partially convincing, as although drinking went down under Prohibition, it didn't stop completely. The public still wanted to buy alcohol, so it continued to be produced, distributed and sold illegally. People like moonshiners and bootleggers made alcohol, while rum-runners smuggled it into America. The public was then able to drink it in speakeasies.
- Interpretation 1 claims that 'the number of crimes and misdemeanors' related to drunkenness 'declined' due to Prohibition. This is partially convincing because fewer crimes linked to alcohol were committed during the 1920s. However, Prohibition also led to a rise in organised crime, as gangs all over the country fought for control over the illegal distribution of alcohol. In Chicago, for example, Al Capone fought other gangsters to run the city's speakeasies. This battle for control led to extreme violence and hundreds of murders, as Capone and his men targeted and killed members of rival gangs.
- Interpretation 2 suggests that people got around Prohibition by drinking in a 'speak-easy' or making their own alcohol. This is convincing because illegal drinking clubs sprang up across the country after Prohibition was introduced. In addition, moonshiners made their own liquor and bootleggers took alcohol that was meant to be used in industry and made it drinkable. This made Prohibition impossible to enforce.
- Interpretation 2 suggests that Prohibition led to otherwise 'respected citizens' breaking the law. This is convincing because Prohibition banned the production, distribution and sale of alcohol, but demand for alcohol remained high. This meant that people had to break the law in order to gain access to alcohol, which they did by either buying it or making it illegally.
- Overall, Interpretation 2 is more convincing because it gives a more balanced view of the impact of Prohibition in America. Sabin acknowledges that saloons disappeared, just like Felix von Luckner, but goes on to consider Prohibition's negative impact too. On the other hand, Felix von Luckner considers the positive impact of Prohibition, but shows very little awareness of the issues that it caused.

4 This question is level marked. How to grade your answer:

Level 1 1-2 marks	The answer shows appropriate knowledge of the period by identifying at least one relevant difficulty.
Level 2 3-4 marks	The answer shows appropriate knowledge and understanding of the period by identifying two relevant difficulties and explaining each one.

Answers

Here are some points your answer may include:
- One difficulty that 'new' immigrants to America faced in the 1920s was poor working and living conditions. This was because many 'new' immigrants were exploited by employers, who made them work long hours for little pay. As a result, many 'new' immigrants could only afford to live in the poorest areas of cities, where conditions were cramped and dirty.
- Another difficulty faced by 'new' immigrants to America in the 1920s was unfair treatment by the justice system. For example, two Italian immigrants called Nicola Sacco and Bartolomeo Vanzetti were executed for murder and robbery in 1927, although there was no clear evidence that they were guilty. Many thought that the men's status as immigrants led the court to discriminate against them.

5   This question is level marked. How to grade your answer:

Level 1 1-2 marks	The answer describes one or more changes, but doesn't explain them. Some knowledge and understanding of the period is shown.
Level 2 3-4 marks	The answer describes some valid changes and explains one of them in more detail. Appropriate knowledge and understanding of the period is shown.
Level 3 5-6 marks	The answer explains two or more changes in detail. A good level of knowledge and understanding of the period is used to support the explanations.
Level 4 7-8 marks	The answer explains more complex patterns of change. Excellent knowledge and understanding of the period is used to support the explanations.

Here are some points your answer may include:
- Many Americans experienced a rise in living standards due to the 'boom' of the 1920s. This was because employment rates were high and wages increased. In addition, hire-purchase allowed people to pay for goods in instalments, and credit was easy to get. This improved people's standard of living as it meant that they could afford expensive goods like hoovers, washing machines and cars.
- The 'boom' of the 1920s enabled some people to get rich by speculating on the stock market. The value of shares in prospering companies kept increasing, prompting people to keep buying shares and leading to a stock market boom. This created an opportunity to make money for some Americans, who bought shares on credit, waited for their value to go up, then sold them on for a profit.
- The car industry grew quickly during the 'boom' of the 1920s, and this led to a huge increase in car ownership. Manufacturers like Ford started using mass production, meaning that cars were built quickly and efficiently on assembly lines. This led to cars becoming more affordable for customers, and millions of Americans owned a car by the end of the decade. The widespread ownership of cars affected people's lives as it meant that they could live further from work. Many people moved to newly-built suburbs on the edge of cities.
- The methods of mass production used in Ford's factories were copied by other industries, meaning that consumer goods like radios and fridges became much more affordable for Americans during the 'boom'. This is because the goods could be made quickly, efficiently and in larger quantities, which drove their prices down. The fact that people could more easily afford consumer goods such as radios and fridges meant that their standard of living improved.

- The 'boom' didn't benefit the lives of everyone in America, such as farmers who were struggling with debt. Some farmers had taken out loans to expand their farms during the First World War, but a fall in demand for food at the end of the war meant that they were unable to repay the loans. In the South, demand for cotton also fell as the textile industry started using man-made synthetic fibres. Many struggling farmers had to sell their farms and travel around the country to find work, and the 'boom' did very little to relieve their poverty.
- Many African Americans still experienced hardship during the 'boom'. For example, many African-American sharecroppers in southern states lived in extreme poverty and suffered from discrimination due to segregation. These conditions forced many African Americans to migrate to the North looking for work, but even then they often still lived in poverty.

6   This question is level marked. How to grade your answer:

Level 1 1-3 marks	The answer shows limited knowledge and understanding of the period. It explains one or both bullet points in a general way.
Level 2 4-6 marks	The answer shows some appropriate knowledge and understanding of the period. It gives a simple analysis of one or both bullet points, using knowledge of the period to justify its points.
Level 3 7-9 marks	The answer shows a good level of appropriate knowledge and understanding of the period. It analyses both bullet points in more detail, using knowledge of the period to justify its points.
Level 4 10-12 marks	The answer shows detailed and precise knowledge and understanding of the period. It analyses both bullet points in detail, using knowledge of the period to justify its points. It makes connections between the bullet points and comes to a clear conclusion about which one was more important.

Here are some points your answer may include:
- The 'boom' that America experienced in the 1920s was an important economic reason for inequalities in America. This 'boom' benefited some people but not others, which increased the gap between the rich and the poor. For some people, employment rates were high and wages increased. Many companies prospered as people had more money to spend on their products, and some people became rich by speculating on the stock market. On the other hand, farmers and people who worked in old industries such as the coal industry struggled to make a living. Therefore, the economic 'boom' created inequality by creating a larger gap between the rich and the poor.
- Inequalities between men and women continued due to economic reasons. Although the position of women in society was starting to change, with women gaining the vote in 1920, many women still faced inequality. This was particularly a problem for poorer women, who were often unable to fight for more rights because they had to focus on surviving. As well as looking after the home, many women were forced to take on extra work to support their families. This shows that the fight for gender equality was limited by economic factors.

- However, inequalities between men and women also existed due to social reasons. For example, African-American women often couldn't vote because of racism and prejudice, meaning that they faced inequality as a result of social attitudes. In addition, women were still expected to raise children, do housework and stick to Victorian morals. These expectations about the role of women contributed to inequality because they meant that women were denied the same opportunities as men.
- Many African Americans experienced inequality for social reasons. African Americans in the South were discriminated against through segregation, which created inequality by making them use separate facilities to white people. However, racism and prejudice were widespread across the whole country. For example, African Americans were targeted by members of the Ku Klux Klan, who wanted to keep America white and Protestant. They were kidnapped, tarred and feathered or even murdered by members of the KKK.
- Many 'new' immigrants to America also suffered from inequality for social reasons. Americans disapproved of 'new' immigrants for a wide range of reasons, such as the fear that some of them were communists who would undermine the American way of life, or the fact that a lot of them were Catholics or Jews who therefore held different beliefs to the mostly Protestant US population. This meant that 'new' immigrants were treated unequally by other Americans, who often viewed them with distrust and suspicion.
- Overall, social reasons were more important than economic reasons in creating inequality in 1920s America. Although the economic 'boom' widened the gap between the rich and the poor, it was groups such as women, African Americans and 'new' immigrants who suffered the most from inequality. These groups were affected by economic factors too, but it was social attitudes towards them that made the inequality that they faced unlikely to change.

Americans' Experiences of the Depression and New Deal

Page 19 — America in the Depression
Knowledge and Understanding
1 a) The constant buying and selling of shares on the stock market inflated their prices, making shares seem more valuable than they really were.
  b) In 1929, people started to realise that businesses were struggling, so they panicked and tried to sell their shares. The rapid selling of shares caused the stock market to collapse.
  c) It became almost impossible to get credit. America's economy relied on credit, so this led to an economic depression.
2 a) Production dropped by a third between 1929 and 1931.
  b) Banks had to close because a lot of Americans couldn't afford to pay back their bank loans and stopped depositing their money in banks.
  c) Many businesses closed. Banks no longer gave credit to people, which meant that people couldn't afford to buy consumer goods. This fall in demand caused a lot of businesses to struggle.

3 Farmers couldn't pay their mortgages as their debts were growing. They were already struggling as a result of overproduction, but the Depression added to the problem by making prices so low that it wasn't worth taking crops and other produce to market. This meant that farmers' debts increased and they didn't have enough income to pay their mortgages. Many farmers were either evicted or forced to become tenant farmers as a result.
4 The term 'Dust Bowl' was used to describe huge areas of land in the Midwest where no crops could be grown due to a long series of droughts. This made the Depression even worse for farmers in the area as many of them had to leave their land and migrate to places such as California to find work. However, work was scarce and they were often exploited by employers.
5 Overproduction was a particularly serious problem for businesses during the Depression because the supply of some goods was already much higher than the demand for them, which meant that businessmen were paying to produce goods that weren't being sold or making a profit. The Depression meant that people had less money to spend, which made public demand for these goods even lower than before.
6 Some businessmen were very wealthy, so they could deal with the loss of income that resulted from the Depression. Other businessmen had invested in areas that weren't so badly affected by the Depression, such as property.

Thinking Historically
1 a) The Depression led to a big drop in employment levels among businessmen and workers. Unemployment had increased to 25% by 1933, compared to 5.5% in 1929. Many people were out of work for years.
  b) There was a large increase in poverty. There was no national welfare system in America, so many people relied on relief from local governments and charities that provided food, clothing and accommodation. It became common to see people queuing for food in 'bread lines'.
  c) The Depression left hundreds of thousands of Americans homeless. There were relief schemes to provide shelter for some of these people, but others were forced to live on the streets.
  d) The Depression disrupted family life. People were forced to delay their marriages and the birth rate also fell. Many families had to leave their homes to seek work, and some fathers abandoned their families in search of work.

Page 21 — Hoover and Roosevelt
Knowledge and Understanding
1 a) The Smoot-Hawley Tariff (1930) raised the price of imported goods to encourage people to buy goods made in America.
  b) The National Credit Corporation was an organisation set up in 1931. It established a loan fund that all major banks were meant to pay into to protect struggling banks from closing.
  c) The Reconstruction Finance Corporation (RFC) was established in 1932. It gave out loans to try to stop businesses and banks from failing.
  d) The Federal Home Loan Bank Act (1932) encouraged banks to offer more mortgages in an attempt to make home ownership cheaper.
2 a) Other countries responded by raising the price of imported US goods. This harmed recovery by causing a fall in trade to and from America.
  b) The scheme failed because most banks didn't want to help their rivals, and thought that the government should create the fund instead.
  c) The RFC failed to give individuals the direct relief that they needed, so it had very little impact.

Answers

d) Many people were still losing their homes. Some of these homeless people were forced to build shanty towns, which became known as 'Hoovervilles'.

Interpretation

1 Sherwood thinks that Hoover had seemed like an ideal candidate to lead the country, saying that he possessed 'exceptional qualifications for the Presidency'. However, he thinks that Hoover 'failed lamentably' to deal with the Depression, and that this led to a loss of 'prestige' and of 'popular faith' in the US government.

2 Sherwood holds Hoover personally responsible for America's problems during the Depression, whereas Allen thinks that Hoover was unfairly blamed for the Depression. Allen admits that Hoover was too optimistic about America's recovery from the Depression, but argues that Hoover was mostly just unfortunate to be in charge when the Depression struck. He suggests that Hoover's biggest mistake was 'getting himself elected'.

3 Here are some points your answer may include:
   - The interpretations might give different views about Hoover's role in the Depression because they were written for different purposes. Sherwood was close to FDR and was writing a biography about him, so is likely to portray him positively by showing that Hoover was responsible for America's problems and that FDR was the one to solve them. In contrast, Allen was writing a general overview of the 1920s as a whole, so is likely to give a more balanced view of the figures involved.
   - The interpretations might give different views about Hoover's role in the Depression due to Sherwood's involvement in FDR's presidency. As a speechwriter for FDR, who opposed Hoover during the 1932 presidential election, Sherwood is highly likely to support FDR and criticise his opponents. Allen wasn't closely involved in the government, so is unlikely to show a strong bias towards either FDR or Hoover.

Page 23 — Roosevelt and the New Deal

Knowledge and Understanding

1 a) The banking system had nearly collapsed and people didn't have confidence in it.
   b) The Emergency Banking Act was passed, which meant that weaker banks were reorganised and supervised by the government.
   c) A law was introduced to make banks take steps to protect people's deposits. As a result, fewer banks failed, deposits started to rise, and people started to regain confidence in the banking system.

2 The fireside chats were radio broadcasts where Roosevelt explained what action the government was taking. They continued throughout his presidency. He did them to increase people's trust in the government after the Depression and to boost people's morale when they were struggling.

3 a) • National Recovery Administration
   • It worked with businesses to reform working practices. It created codes to try to ensure fair competition, set minimum wages and maximum working hours, and encouraged trade unions.
   b) • Federal Emergency Relief Administration
   • It provided money to state and local governments to allow them to supply emergency relief. It funded relief payments for the unemployed and provided direct support for the poor, such as soup kitchens.
   c) • Civilian Conservation Corps
   • It paid thousands of unemployed young men to do work in forestry, water and soil conservation projects. It had given work to more than 3 million people by June 1942.

d) • Agricultural Adjustment Administration
   • It paid farmers to limit their food production, causing prices and incomes to rise. It reformed agriculture by helping farmers to modernise and rebuild their farms.

4 a) It gave a government pension to Americans over the age of 65. It also gave unemployment benefit to people who lost their job and set up schemes to help the sick, the disabled and poor children.
   b) It gave workers the right to join trade unions without the risk of being sacked. It also created the National Labor Relations Board to resolve disagreements between employers and unions. However, some workers, like farmers, weren't covered by the act.
   c) It created work for over 8.5 million people, including jobs in construction and the arts.
   d) It settled families on government farms and gave advice on farming to them. It later helped tenant farmers to apply for loans so that they could buy their own land.

5 The First New Deal aimed to provide temporary relief to people who were suffering from the social and economic consequences of the Depression. In contrast, the Second New Deal aimed to improve people's health and well-being in the long term. It set the foundations for a welfare state in America.

Page 25 — New Deal Opposition and Criticism

Knowledge and Understanding

1 a) Congress is a group of elected politicians who hold power in America alongside the President and the Supreme Court.
   b) The Constitution is a set of laws. The powers of the President, Congress and the Supreme Court are laid down in the Constitution.
   c) The Supreme Court is the most powerful court in America. It has nine judges who are chosen by the President and politicians. They judge cases linked to the Constitution and laws that apply in every state.

2 Roosevelt wanted to add more Democrats to the Supreme Court to make it more likely to support him. The Supreme Court contained Republicans who had opposed his policies and declared some parts of the New Deal unconstitutional, as well as closing agencies like the NRA and the AAA.

3 a) Supreme Court judges opposed the New Deal because they thought that it involved FDR taking power that the Constitution hadn't given to him.
   b) Some left-wing politicians opposed the New Deal because they thought that it didn't go far enough. Senator Huey Long wanted FDR to go further by taxing rich people and giving every family $2000 a year. On the other hand, Republicans thought that the New Deal had gone too far, taxing the rich too much and spending too much money.
   c) Many businessmen and industrialists didn't think that the government should have the power to interfere in business, such as by supporting unions. Many of them were against higher taxes and wages under the New Deal.

4 a) The CCC segregated African-American workers, and the NRA allowed African-American workers to be paid less than white workers for doing the same job.
   b) New Deal agencies often focused on helping men, and women were often paid less than men.

Answers

Thinking Historically

1 You can choose any group, as long as you explain your answer. For example:
Opposition from the Supreme Court might have concerned Roosevelt the most, because it was the most powerful court in America. It actively tried to undermine the New Deal, whereas politicians only criticised the New Deal without taking concrete action. Other opponents like businessmen and industrialists criticised Roosevelt and set up organisations like the American Liberty League to oppose him, but they didn't have the power to declare his policies unconstitutional or to close down New Deal agencies like the Supreme Court did.

2 a) • The New Deal provided direct relief for those suffering from poverty and unemployment. The FERA provided support to the poor, for example in soup kitchens, and funded relief payments to those who were out of work.
   • The New Deal improved the social welfare of the most vulnerable people in society. The 1935 Social Security Act provided a state pension for people over the age of 65, and unemployment benefit for people who had lost their job. It also set up other schemes to help the sick, the disabled and poor children.
   • The New Deal had long-term social consequences. By bringing in social welfare reforms, it set the foundations for a welfare state and changed the way that Americans viewed the duties of the federal government.

   b) • The New Deal restored confidence in the banking system. The 1933 Emergency Banking Act saw the government start to reorganise and supervise weaker banks. In addition, the government made banks take steps to protect people's deposits. As a result, fewer banks failed and confidence in banking grew.
   • The New Deal helped to reduce unemployment levels. The CCC gave paid work to thousands of unemployed young men, and the WPA gave a wide range of different jobs to more than 8.5 million people. The fact that more people were working and earning money helped the economic recovery.
   • The New Deal reformed agriculture. The AAA paid farmers to limit production, which meant that prices and incomes increased. It also helped farmers to modernise and rebuild their farms. The AAA's work was taken over by the FSA after it ended in 1935.

3 You can choose any opinion, as long as you explain your answer. For example:
The New Deal was only partially successful. The social changes that it introduced had a significant impact both in the short term and the long term, as it provided relief from the social consequences of the Depression before putting measures in place to improve social welfare in the future. However, the economic changes brought in by the New Deal had less of an impact. Many of the jobs created were only temporary, and industry didn't completely pick up again until the Second World War.

Page 27 — 1930s Popular Culture
Knowledge and Understanding

1 • Musicals
 • Comedies
 • Horror Films
 • Fantasy Films
 • Gangster Films

2 Musicals featured glamorous stars, such as Fred Astaire and Ginger Rogers, in decadent settings. This provided a contrast to the difficult conditions that most people were experiencing in their everyday lives during the Depression.

3 In 1930s America, a lot of music was optimistic, delivering hopeful messages to Americans who were struggling. The song that Roosevelt used as a theme tune for his presidential campaign, 'Happy Days Are Here Again', remained popular throughout the decade. Also, new genres became popular, such as swing music, which was up-tempo and easy to dance to. People could listen to music on the radio, which also became very popular in the 1930s.

4 Some famous swing musicians, such as Duke Ellington, were African-American. The bands that they played in were often segregated, as were the audiences, but some bands started to feature black and white musicians by the mid-1930s.

5 The Depression meant that people couldn't afford tickets to baseball games, so attendance fell. This forced teams to cut players' wages. In response, baseball teams started playing games at night when people weren't at work in an attempt to get more people to attend.

6 Woody Guthrie was a folk singer who sang about the hardship suffered by Dust Bowl migrants and workers. He had fled the Dust Bowl himself, staying in migrants camps on the way to California in search of work. As a result, his music was very political and often focused on his personal experiences.

Thinking Historically

1 a) • A novel by John Steinbeck about a family leaving their farm in the Dust Bowl.
   • Many farmers were forced to flee the Dust Bowl after a long series of droughts. They were forced to roam around the country in search of work.
   b) • A novel by Richard Wright about oppressed African Americans facing discrimination in the ghettos of Chicago.
   • Discrimination forced African Americans to live in ghettos in the poorest areas of cities. These ghettos were usually run-down and overcrowded.
   c) • A film about a struggling factory worker, which depicts widespread unemployment, poverty and homelessness in America.
   • By 1933, 25% of America's workforce was unemployed. This led to problems such as poverty and homelessness. Workers in factories were particularly badly affected, as industrial production dropped by a third between 1929 and 1931, causing wage cuts and job losses.

Page 29 — Economic Impact of World War Two
Knowledge and Understanding

1 America didn't join the fighting because many Americans didn't want to get involved in another war.

2 When the Second World War broke out, America was still suffering from the effects of the Depression. Although the New Deal had provided economic stability, many people were still suffering from unemployment and poverty. 16% of Americans were still without a job in 1939, compared to 5.5% of Americans in 1929.

3 The Lend-Lease programme was a scheme introduced in 1941 to provide support to the Allies during the war. The US government bought military supplies from US manufacturers to send to the countries fighting against Germany, especially the UK and the USSR.

4 The Lend-Lease programme boosted the US economy by increasing the production of military supplies, like weapons, ships and planes. America didn't charge the Allies for any goods that were used up or destroyed during the war, but the increase in production stimulated industry and reduced unemployment.

Answers

5
- Food
- Coal
- Timber
- Clothing
- Chemicals

6   America entered the war because Japan carried out a surprise attack on the US Navy at Pearl Harbor in Hawaii, killing around 2400 Americans.

Thinking Historically

1 a)   There was an increase in the production of military supplies such as weapons, planes, tanks and trucks. The War Production Board was set up in order to oversee this increase in production. New factories were established, and existing factories were converted to start making military supplies. For example, factories that usually made metal goods such as nails switched to making bullets and shells.

  b)   Millions of people were employed in industry to meet the demands of the war, while millions of others went to join the armed forces. This ended the mass unemployment of the 1930s, and there was even a shortage of factory workers by the end of 1943. There was also a shortage of farm workers, as many of them had been drafted into the Army or had found better paid jobs in factories.

  c)   An increase in employment levels and in the demand for workers across the country caused wages to go up.

2   You can answer either way, as long as you explain your answer. For example:
The Second World War was more important in ending the Depression. It was only once America joined the fighting that the aims of Roosevelt's New Deal were fully achieved. With millions of people joining the armed forces and millions more working in industry to produce military supplies, there was high employment and wages started to grow. This helped to solve serious problems such as mass unemployment and poverty, which the New Deal had started to tackle, but failed to bring to an end.

Page 31 — Social Impact of World War Two
Knowledge and Understanding

1   More women were working before the Second World War broke out because the Depression had led to a lot of men losing their jobs, leaving them unable to support their families. This meant that both men and women had to seek work. However, women were limited to typically 'female' jobs like teaching, nursing and cleaning, and most of them were paid less than men. They were also criticised for taking jobs away from men, and suffered discrimination from New Deal agencies.

2 a)   The WAVES replaced US Navy officers and seamen who worked on shore. They worked in a wide range of roles, including as doctors, engineers and radio operators.

  b)   The WASPS flew Air Force planes in non-combat roles to allow male pilots to fight abroad.

  c)   Members of the WAC worked in several roles within the US Army, including as mechanics, switchboard operators, typists and office clerks.

  d)   Members of the WLA volunteered to work on farms during the war.

Interpretation

1 a)   Hahne suggests that women were expected to give up their war-time jobs to men and return to their domestic roles once the war ended. She says that women were meant to go home 'cheerfully'.

  b)   Hahne suggests that women resisted these expectations, as they enjoyed the freedom granted to them by working and earning their own money. She says that women had 'a taste of freedom' and didn't want to give it up after the war.

  c)   Hahne suggests that developments during World War Two set the foundations for the women's rights movement. She says that the movement 'had its seeds' during the war and its aftermath.

2   You can answer either way, as long as you explain your answer. For example:
The interpretation is convincing as many women still wanted to work at the end of the Second World War. Although women were widely expected to give up their war-time jobs to men and return to domestic roles at the end of the war, the number of women in work had already increased again by the early 1950s. This shows that many women wanted to keep working, even though the war no longer demanded it.

Page 33 — Social Impact of World War Two
Knowledge and Understanding

1   Executive Order 8802 formed the Fair Employment Practice Committee and made it illegal to discriminate against defence workers because of their race. Roosevelt signed it after Civil Rights campaigners threatened to stage massive protests in Washington. He wanted to avoid the disruption and embarrassment that these protests might have caused.

2   Some African Americans started to question whether they should fight for the freedoms of Europeans when America didn't give the same freedoms to them.

3 a)   'Double Victory' was a campaign set up by Civil Rights activists that encouraged African Americans to fight for their own democratic rights in America as well as fighting for democracy in Europe. The aim was to earn one victory over enemies outside America (e.g. Hitler), and another victory over enemies inside the country (e.g. opponents of racial equality in America).

  b)   CORE was the Congress of Racial Equality, an organisation set up in 1942. It protested against segregation using non-violent methods that were strongly influenced by Mahatma Gandhi's philosophy of non-violence.

4   CORE influenced the Civil Rights movement by using forms of non-violent protest (e.g. sit-ins) that went on to be used regularly in the 1950s and 1960s. CORE's philosophy of non-violence was also echoed by important figures in the Civil Rights movement, such as Martin Luther King.

5
- 1940 — A law is passed making it illegal to discriminate against African Americans in army recruitment. However, there are still limits on the number of black men who are able to enlist and segregation continues.
- 1943 — All leisure facilities are desegregated.
- 1944 — All army transport buses are desegregated.
- 1946 — African Americans are banned from enlisting. Civil Rights activists ask the government to reverse the decision.
- 1948 — American Civil Rights activists protest against segregation in the US Army. They gain support from President Truman, who desegregates the US Army by signing Executive Order 9981 in July 1948.

Thinking Historically

1 a)   It becomes illegal to discriminate against defence workers because of their race. African Americans are given equal opportunities to work in defence industries.

  b)   This creates racial tension in northern cities. Many white people don't want to compete with black people for work.

  c)   There are housing shortages, and many African Americans are forced to live in poor conditions. They also suffer from prejudice from white workers, who go on strike when black workers are promoted. These tensions lead to a race riot in 1943, in which 25 African Americans and 9 white people are killed.

Answers

2   The Army's policy of 'segregation without discrimination' failed because African-American soldiers still suffered from discrimination. They had worse training and worse living and working conditions. They were also often limited to non-combat roles like building roads and transporting supplies.

Pages 36-37 — Exam-Style Questions

1   This question is level marked. How to grade your answer:

Level 1
1-2 marks
The answer gives differences which are supported by some analysis of one or both interpretations.

Level 2
3-4 marks
The answer explains differences which are well supported by analysis of both interpretations.

Here are some points your answer may include:
- Interpretation 1 suggests that the New Deal failed to have a positive impact because it was badly organised. Kennedy claims that government agencies such as the NRA and the WPA would 'come and go' and says that there was a lack of 'clear-cut decisions'. On the other hand, Interpretation 2 argues that the New Deal did have a positive impact because a lot of work was successfully completed. Eleanor Roosevelt claims that 'innumerable' projects were finished, leaving 'tangible results'.
- Interpretation 1 argues that the disorganised nature of the New Deal held America back. Kennedy claims that there was 'bedlam and confusion in Washington', and that this stopped the country from making the 'progress' of which it was capable. On the other hand, Interpretation 2 suggests that America made a lot of progress under the New Deal. Eleanor Roosevelt claims that the success of various New Deal agencies 'pulled the country out of the depression' and made it possible for America to fight in the Second World War.

2   This question is level marked. How to grade your answer:

Level 1
1-2 marks
The answer gives appropriate reasons why the interpretations are different. The reasons are based on a simple analysis of the interpretations' provenance.

Level 2
3-4 marks
The answer gives appropriate reasons why the interpretations are different. The reasons are well supported by knowledge of the period and a detailed analysis of the interpretations' provenance.

Here are some points your answer may include:
- The authors might have different views because they had different political beliefs. FDR was a Democrat, but Kennedy worked in the US Treasury for Republican President Richard Nixon from 1969 to 1971. Therefore, Kennedy would be more likely to highlight the flaws in FDR's policies. In contrast, Eleanor Roosevelt supported FDR's work on the New Deal in her role as First Lady of the USA from 1933 to 1945. She is likely to have shared FDR's political views, and would therefore be more likely to defend his policies.
- The authors might have different views because they had different perspectives on the Depression and the New Deal. Kennedy worked for America's central bank during the Depression, so he would have been well placed to comment on its economic impact. However, he wouldn't necessarily have been aware of the positive impact that the New Deal was having on people around the country. In contrast, Eleanor Roosevelt saw the progress of the New Deal with her own eyes when travelling around America. This makes her more likely to judge the impact of the New Deal based on her first-hand knowledge of how it improved people's lives.

3   This question is level marked. How to grade your answer:

Level 1
1-2 marks
The answer shows support for one or both interpretations. It is based on a simple analysis of the interpretations and basic knowledge of the topic.

Level 2
3-4 marks
The answer evaluates the credibility of one interpretation. It is supported by a more detailed analysis of the interpretations and some relevant knowledge of the topic.

Level 3
5-6 marks
The answer evaluates the credibility of both interpretations and gives a judgement about which one is more convincing. It is supported by a detailed analysis of the interpretations and a good level of relevant knowledge of the topic.

Level 4
7-8 marks
The answer evaluates the credibility of both interpretations and comes to a clear judgement about which one is more convincing. It is supported by a strong analysis of the interpretations and a wide range of relevant knowledge of the topic.

Here are some points your answer may include:
- Interpretation 1 suggests that the New Deal had a limited impact because government agencies would 'come and go'. This is convincing because FDR introduced a huge number of federal agencies, such as the FERA and the CCC, during the 'Hundred Days'. Some of these agencies, such as the NRA and the AAA, were shut down only two years later after the Supreme Court declared parts of the New Deal unconstitutional. This supports the claim that agencies would 'come and go'.
- Interpretation 1 suggests that New Deal agencies failed to make much progress after some initial success, with Kennedy becoming 'disenchanted' with FDR during his second term. This is only partially convincing. Although the First New Deal only offered temporary solutions to people's problems, which might not have lasted later into FDR's presidency, the Second New Deal had a more long-term impact. Measures like the Social Security Act laid the foundations for a welfare state and changed how Americans saw the duties of the federal government.
- Interpretation 2 suggests that New Deal agencies did 'a collective good' in America. This is partially convincing because many of the federal agencies introduced by FDR helped to combat the economic and social impact of the Depression. For example, the CCC had provided paid work for more than 3 million people by June 1942. However, not all of these agencies did a 'collective good', because some of them discriminated against women and African Americans. The NRA allowed black workers to be paid less than white workers for doing the same work, and other New Deal agencies like the FERA and the WPA paid women less than men.
- Interpretation 2 suggests that New Deal agencies 'pulled the country out of the depression'. This is partially convincing because the agencies helped to reduce problems like unemployment and stopped the economy from collapsing. However, although unemployment fell under the New Deal, FDR's agencies failed to bring back the low unemployment levels of the 1920s. They also did little to revive industry. In reality, it was the Second World War, not New Deal agencies, that lifted America out of the Depression.

Answers

- Overall, Interpretation 2 is more convincing because the New Deal made important progress towards stabilising the economy and providing people with jobs, even if some of the changes were temporary or didn't benefit everyone. Although Eleanor Roosevelt goes too far in saying that New Deal agencies 'pulled the country out of the depression', the Second New Deal in particular did have a positive long-term impact on the lives of Americans. This long-term impact contradicts Kennedy's suggestion that FDR's New Deal agencies failed to deliver positive change after his first two terms in office, making Interpretation 1 less convincing.

4   This question is level marked. How to grade your answer:

Level 1 1-2 marks	The answer shows appropriate knowledge of the period by identifying at least one relevant difficulty.
Level 2 3-4 marks	The answer shows appropriate knowledge and understanding of the period by identifying two relevant difficulties and explaining each one.

Here are some points your answer may include:

- One difficulty that the Republican Party faced was a loss of support in Congress and a loss of public confidence in their ability to lead the country. This was due to the Republican Party's inadequate response to the failure of banks and businesses, and rising levels of poverty, unemployment and homelessness.
- The Republican Party faced the difficulty that the public saw Hoover's refusal to directly support people in need as heartless. As a result, Hoover became very unpopular and was associated with the negative consequences of the Depression. For example, the shanty towns built by homeless people were known as 'Hoovervilles'.
- One difficulty that the Republican Party faced was that FDR's opposition was very effective. FDR proposed a 'New Deal' to improve people's lives, rebuild US trade and industry and create social and economic reforms. This made FDR very popular and meant that his Democratic Party easily defeated the Republican Party in the 1932 election.

5   This question is level marked. How to grade your answer:

Level 1 1-2 marks	The answer describes one or more changes, but doesn't explain them. Some knowledge and understanding of the period is shown.
Level 2 3-4 marks	The answer describes some valid changes and explains one of them in more detail. Appropriate knowledge and understanding of the period is shown.
Level 3 5-6 marks	The answer explains two or more changes in detail. A good level of knowledge and understanding of the period is used to support the explanations.
Level 4 7-8 marks	The answer explains more complex patterns of change. Excellent knowledge and understanding of the period is used to support the explanations.

Here are some points your answer may include:

- The war effort led to an increase in job opportunities for Americans. Before America joined the war, Lend-Lease helped to reduce unemployment by increasing the production of war supplies, creating a lot of demand for workers. The need for military supplies was even greater after America joined the war in December 1941, which meant that millions of new jobs became available. This brought an end to mass unemployment.

- The war effort helped women to gain new opportunities. Women were often limited to typically 'female' jobs like nursing and teaching before the war. However, there was a shortage of workers in America due to a large increase in industrial production and the drafting of male workers into the Army. This meant that women were needed in a wider range of roles. Millions of women started to work in skilled jobs in factories, shipyards and defence facilities.
- The war effort affected the lives of African Americans by giving them access to jobs that they had been excluded from before the Second World War. In June 1941, the demand for defence workers to help the war effort encouraged FDR to sign Executive Order 8802, which banned racial discrimination in defence industries. Thousands of black workers took advantage of these new opportunities by migrating to northern cities, where they also earned higher wages than they would have earned in the South.
- The war effort had a positive impact on farmers' lives by helping their incomes to return to pre-Depression levels. America started to export more food to Europe in order to meet an increase in demand from the Allies. This increase in demand drove food prices up, which allowed farmers to make more money.
- The war effort led to Americans having more money to spend. This was because wages rose due to high employment levels and high demand for workers across the country. The rise in wages meant that more Americans had more money to spend on goods, which helped to improve their standard of living.

6   This question is level marked. How to grade your answer:

Level 1 1-3 marks	The answer shows limited knowledge and understanding of the period. It explains one or both bullet points in a general way.
Level 2 4-6 marks	The answer shows some appropriate knowledge and understanding of the period. It gives a simple analysis of one or both bullet points, using knowledge of the period to justify its points.
Level 3 7-9 marks	The answer shows a good level of appropriate knowledge and understanding of the period. It analyses both bullet points in more detail, using knowledge of the period to justify its points.
Level 4 10-12 marks	The answer shows detailed and precise knowledge and understanding of the period. It analyses both bullet points in detail, using knowledge of the period to justify its points. It makes connections between the bullet points and comes to a clear conclusion about which one was more important.

Here are some points your answer may include:

- The Depression had serious consequences for America's economy. For example, there was a significant fall in industrial production. Between 1929 and 1931, industrial production decreased by a third. This meant that bosses were forced to cut wages and sack workers.
- One economic consequence of the Depression was that the banks started to struggle. Many Americans couldn't afford to pay back bank loans, and they stopped depositing money in the bank. This forced many banks to close, and led to people's savings being lost. In addition, the remaining banks no longer gave credit to customers.

Answers

- The failure of the banking system had consequences for businesses. The lack of availability of credit meant that people didn't have enough money to buy consumer goods, which caused demand for these goods to fall. This lack of demand forced businesses to close.
- Another economic consequence of the Depression was that farming became less profitable and farmers' debts increased. Overproduction was already a problem for farmers after the First World War, but the Depression made it worse. The price of food and other produce was so low that it often wasn't worth taking them to market. Many farms failed due to the loss of income, as farmers were unable to repay their mortgages.
- One of the social consequences of America's economic difficulties was mass unemployment. Many businesses went bankrupt and were forced to close, which caused business owners and their workers to lose their jobs. Only 5.5% of workers were without a job in 1929, but this had risen to 25% by 1939. In addition, many farm workers became unemployed due to the difficulties faced by US farms. They roamed the country looking for jobs, but work was hard to find and they were often exploited by employers.
- Mass unemployment had other social consequences. For example, many Americans suffered from poverty, starvation and homelessness. There was no national welfare system in America at the time, so people were forced to rely on relief schemes. However, these relief schemes were unable to help everyone, and most people continued to suffer. For example, hundreds of thousands of Americans became homeless and were forced to sleep on the streets.
- Another social consequence of the Depression was that family life was disrupted. Some families were forced to leave their homes and move elsewhere in the country to find work, and some fathers even abandoned their families in search of a job. In addition, some people delayed their marriages until their financial situations improved, and the birth rate fell.
- Many of the social consequences of the Depression were linked to the economic difficulties that America was experiencing at the time. Problems such as poverty, unemployment and homelessness had an important impact on America, but they were largely caused by the economic consequences of the Depression.

Post-War America

Page 39 — Post-War Prosperity

Knowledge and Understanding

1   The Second World War had caused an increase in wages and employment, and wages continued to increase until the 1970s. Industry also prospered after the war, meaning that there were lots of goods, like fridges and dishwashers, available to buy. More people could afford these goods, so high demand further boosted the economy. The Cold War also had a positive impact on the US economy, because it led to an increase in military spending and investment in newer industries, like nuclear technology and space exploration and research. This created even more jobs.

2   The Servicemen's Readjustment Act (or 'G.I. Bill') was a policy introduced by Roosevelt in 1944, which offered free college tuition to veterans and gave them loans to help them to buy a home.

Thinking Historically

1 a) There was a rise in consumerism, which meant that a lot of goods were available to buy, and a lot of people were able to afford them. Goods like fridges and dishwashers gave a better standard of living to those who bought them, and luxury goods such as televisions and record players made people's lives more comfortable.

  b) Many of the new houses built as part of the house-building boom were built in the suburbs, which were large housing estates on the edges of towns and cities. People aspired to live in these suburbs, and many of them moved from urban and rural areas to do so. This allowed them to raise their families away from crowded, 'unsafe' cities and live more comfortably.

  c) The growth of suburbia and a high demand for consumer goods led to impressive shopping malls being built in the suburbs. These malls gave people an accessible place to shop and socialise.

Interpretation

1   Harrington suggests that America's post-war prosperity didn't benefit everyone. He describes the isolation of poor people who stayed in the 'central area' of cities while other people moved to the suburbs. He also suggests that the inhabitants of suburbs were unaware of the inequality that America's post-war prosperity created, saying that they only ever got the 'merest glimpse' of the poverty that some people were experiencing.

2   Here are some points your answer may include:
- Harrington might give these views because he was writing a study of poverty in America. This means that he is likely to have witnessed the poor conditions that some Americans were living in, making him more likely to focus on people who didn't benefit from America's post-war prosperity.
- Harrington might give these views because he was a political activist who criticised capitalism for creating inequality. This means that he is more likely to focus on the negative side to America's post-war prosperity.

3   You can answer either way, as long as you explain your answer. For example:
Overall, the interpretation is convincing because it gives a balanced view of America's post-war prosperity. Many Americans benefited from the country's prosperity and had a higher standard of living as a result, like the 'middle-class women' from suburbia mentioned in the interpretation. However, around 25% of the population still lived in poverty, particularly in inner-city areas. The interpretation shows awareness of the difference between richer and poorer people, referring to a range of different groups who lived in 'miserable' conditions in the 'central area'.

Page 41 — Post-War Popular Culture

Knowledge and Understanding

1
- The strength of the post-war economy meant that people had more money to spend on popular culture. On average, Americans had five times as much money to spend on things like music and cinema in 1955 as they did in 1940.
- The development of new technologies, such as television, led to entertainment becoming more accessible than ever before.

2   Americans were expected to marry early and have children. Women were mostly viewed as wives and mothers, so they were expected to stay at home. Families were expected to stick to American values like patriotism, faith and morality.

Answers

3 The fear of communism encouraged people to make films and TV programmes that conformed to American values in an attempt to protect the American way of life. For example, Hollywood made traditional films such as westerns and musicals. Filmmakers also avoided difficult or controversial topics to prevent suspicion that they were communists.

4 It was a genre of music that developed from the blues and country music in the 1950s. It was energetic, loud and aggressive, and it encouraged freedom and defiance. It was designed to appeal to young people.

5 a) Elvis Presley was a rock and roll singer who became an icon of the genre. He was popular among some people for his good looks, suggestive dancing and daring lyrics, but others thought that his music encouraged teenagers to behave in a way that went against American values.

b) James Dean was an actor who starred in films such as 'Rebel Without a Cause' and became a post-war icon. Many young people were able to relate to the frustrated persona and disregard for authority often shown by his characters, but adults thought that he was an unsuitable role model.

Thinking Historically

1 • As more families bought televisions, other forms of entertainment like the cinema became less popular.
• Television made entertainment more accessible. Around 50 million households had a television by 1960.
• TV programmes like 'Leave it to Beaver' and 'Father Knows Best' portrayed idealised and wholesome families. This encouraged the families who watched to uphold traditional American values.
• The widespread popularity of television meant that lots of people watched the same TV programmes, which encouraged large parts of the population to conform to the same values.
• The popularity of television allowed TV advertising to become more widespread, encouraging people to buy more goods.

2 A separate 'teenage' culture developed in the 1950s because the period of post-war prosperity meant that teenagers had more money and free time than ever before. 1950s American society was also based on conforming to traditional values, which might have made teenagers more likely to want to rebel against it.

3 Older generations might have opposed the development of a separate 'teenage' culture in the 1950s because this 'teenage' culture was based on the idea of rebelling against conformity and adult authority. In a society that emphasised the importance of values like morality, older generations worried that things like rock and roll music encouraged immoral behaviour like crime and rebellion among young people.

Page 43 — McCarthyism

Knowledge and Understanding

1 America and the USSR were 'ideologically opposed' to each other as America was capitalist, but the USSR was communist. America had a democratically elected government, but the USSR was a single-party state. The countries also had different views on the economy. America's economy was based on private ownership of property, free competition and the forces of supply and demand, while the USSR's economy was controlled by the government, with no private ownership of property.

2 Tension between America and the USSR led to a Cold War from 1945 to 1991. At this time, a climate of fear about the influence of communism started to grow in America, causing a second 'Red Scare'. The USSR's creation of a sphere of influence in Eastern Europe and North Korea's invasion of South Korea gave Americans the impression that communism was spreading and becoming more powerful, which added further to this climate of fear.

3 Some US politicians thought that communists were hostile to American values and wanted to destroy American society. There was a growing fear that, if communists were allowed to work for the US government, they would try to undermine it from the inside.

4 Senator McCarthy claimed that he had a list of 205 communists working in the US State Department, and that some of these communists were putting America at risk by giving information to the USSR.

5 McCarthy's anti-communist stance made him popular with voters, which increased his political power.

6 • He made accusations with little evidence.
• He intimidated witnesses.
• He encouraged people to accuse others.

7 People might have been reluctant to criticise McCarthy because there was a risk that they would be accused of being communist sympathisers.

Thinking Historically

1 a) Margaret Chase Smith and the other Republicans were some of the first people to speak out against McCarthy's tactics at a time when people were scared of being accused of being communist sympathisers. This might have encouraged more people to speak out against McCarthy and his tactics.

b) Edward Murrow's criticism of McCarthy on 'See It Now' was televised, so his claim that McCarthy's 'witch-hunts' were a greater threat to society than communism might have been seen by a lot of people. This might have helped to turn public opinion against McCarthy.

c) The fact that the Army-McCarthy hearings were shown on TV meant that people could see McCarthy's bullying of witnesses first-hand. This made him unpopular with the public, and the Senate expressed its disapproval by voting to censure him later in the same year.

2 You can choose any event, as long as you explain your answer. For example:
The Army-McCarthy hearings were most significant in causing McCarthy's downfall because they allowed people to see McCarthy's tactics for themselves. These tactics had been criticised before by people like Margaret Chase Smith and Edward Murrow, but the hearings confirmed that these criticisms were accurate. This is what caused McCarthy to lose popularity with the general public and led the Senate to censure him.

Page 45 — Segregation

Knowledge and Understanding

1 a) Jim Crow Laws were laws that were introduced to southern states from the late 19th century. They segregated white and black Americans in workplaces, schools, restaurants and a wide range of other public facilities.

b) The phrase 'separate but equal' refers to a doctrine created in 1890 to justify racial segregation. It included the idea that the separate facilities provided for African Americans were meant to be equal in quality to the facilities used by white Americans.

2 The 15th Amendment is an amendment to the US Constitution that was introduced in 1870. It says that no US citizen should be denied the right to vote because of their race or colour.

3 a) People had to pay poll taxes in order to vote, but poorer African Americans couldn't afford to pay.

b) Only people who owned property over a certain value were able to vote. Few African Americans owned property that was valuable enough to meet the requirements.

c) The tests were often carried out by white officials who deliberately failed black entrants.

4 It made it very difficult for African-American defendants to get a fair trial in a southern court.

5 a) Homeowners' associations discouraged selling houses in white communities to African Americans, which forced them to live in run-down and overcrowded neighbourhoods.

b) African Americans were often restricted to unskilled jobs which were badly paid.

Thinking Historically

1 a) It was difficult for African Americans to get a good education in the South because schools were segregated, and African-American schools relied on white-controlled local governments for funding. This meant that African-American schools often received less money than white schools. As a result, most African-American schools were overcrowded, had poor-quality buildings and lacked books and other resources. This put African Americans at a disadvantage by giving them a worse education than white people.

b) African Americans had limited employment opportunities. They were barred from skilled jobs in industry and from most professional and office jobs. This meant that most African Americans worked as farm labourers. This work was unskilled and badly paid.

c) Many African Americans were unable to vote due to racist laws, which meant that they had no voice in politics. This helped to maintain segregation in the South because it meant that southern state governments were dominated by the Democratic Party, which supported segregation. These southern Democrats were also powerful in the national government, allowing them to block attempts to get rid of segregation and give African Americans equal rights.

Page 47 — The Civil Rights Movement
Knowledge and Understanding

1 • 1954 — The Supreme Court rules in the case Brown v Board of Education of Topeka that racial segregation in schools is unconstitutional. As a result, southern states are supposed to desegregate their public schools.

• 1955 — Rosa Parks is arrested after refusing to give up her seat on a bus to a white passenger in Montgomery, Alabama. Martin Luther King and other black ministers organise a bus boycott in protest, which lasts for more than a year. Protesters are violently attacked, and four churches and King's home are bombed, but the Supreme Court eventually rules that Alabama's bus segregation laws are unconstitutional.

• 1957 — Nine African-American students are confronted by an angry mob on their first day at Little Rock Central High School in Arkansas. Orval Faubus, the state governor, sends the National Guard to keep the students out. President Eisenhower intervenes by sending the US Army to enforce desegregation.

• 1960 — A group of black and white college students stage sit-ins at the segregated lunch counter in a Woolworths department store in Greensboro, North Carolina. After several months of protests, the lunch counter is successfully desegregated.

• 1961 — Protesters start challenging segregation on interstate bus services. Groups of black and white Americans board interstate buses in the North, where they are desegregated, and travel together to southern states, where segregation is enforced. The protesters are attacked by violent mobs and arrested by local authorities. In response, the federal government issues a desegregation order on all interstate buses and trains.

• 1963 — Governor Wallace blocks black students from enrolling at the University of Alabama. Kennedy takes control of Alabama's National Guard and orders them to make sure the students are admitted.

2 It was difficult to enforce desegregation in public schools after Brown v Board of Education of Topeka because state authorities often tried to defy the Supreme Court's ruling. The lack of a national Civil Rights law made it difficult for the federal government to enforce desegregation in individual states.

3 The NAACP was the National Association for the Advancement of Colored People, an organisation which aimed to achieve equality for all in America. It funded several important court cases that involved challenging discrimination and campaigned for racial equality.

Thinking Historically

1 a) It weakened the legal basis for Jim Crow Laws in the South and inspired Civil Rights activists to challenge discrimination in other areas.

b) The success of the non-violent boycott inspired others who opposed segregation in the South.

c) They inspired other sit-ins. By April 1960, it was estimated that over 50,000 students had participated in a sit-in. Many of the sit-ins inspired by the one in Greensboro were also successful in forcing desegregation.

d) The widespread violence caused by opposition to the Freedom Rides forced Kennedy to intervene. This led to the federal government issuing a desegregation order on all interstate buses and trains across the country.

2 You can choose any of the events, as long as you explain your answer. For example:
The Brown v Board of Education of Topeka ruling was most significant because it provided a legal basis for Civil Rights activists to challenge segregation, therefore justifying the actions of protesters who took part in protests such as the Montgomery Bus Boycott, the Greensboro Sit-Ins and the Freedom Rides. The ruling was also inspirational to Civil Rights activists across America, who might not have taken part in these later protests if the NAACP's campaign hadn't succeeded.

Page 49 — Martin Luther King and Malcolm X
Knowledge and Understanding

1 a) • Martin Luther King believed in non-violence. He thought that it would help to create understanding between white people and African Americans.

• Malcolm X thought that African Americans should use 'any means necessary', including violence, to achieve equality.

b) • King supported the integration of white and black people in US society.

• Malcolm X believed in black separatism. He thought that black people should give up on integration and form their own separate nation if they failed to gain freedom, justice and equality in US society.

c) • King didn't want to treat white people as the enemy.

• Malcolm X saw white people as the enemy and condemned them for their role in oppressing African Americans.

2 After leaving the Nation of Islam, Malcolm X moved away from black separatism and started to preach non-violence.

Answers

3 a) The protesters are arrested, including Martin Luther King.

   b) A desegregation agreement is reached, which some white people oppose.

   c) Some African Americans start rioting in response to King being targeted by bombers.

4   Martin Luther King and the SCLC organised a huge march on Washington DC on 28th August 1963, which was attended by a crowd of more than 250,000 people. During the march, King gave his famous 'I Have a Dream' speech, in which he called for an end to racism in America. The march received huge media attention and showed that there was a lot of support for the Civil Rights movement, putting pressure on Congress to pass Kennedy's Civil Rights bill.

5   • Its members went on armed patrol to defend African Americans from police violence.

    • It carried out education programmes.

    • It carried out healthcare programmes.

Thinking Historically

1 a) Martin Luther King played an important role in pushing for meaningful Civil Rights laws that improved the lives of African Americans. He was involved in marches and sit-ins in Birmingham in 1963, which persuaded Kennedy to take strong action on Civil Rights by presenting a Civil Rights bill to Congress. King then went on to organise the March on Washington, which put pressure on Congress to pass Kennedy's Civil Rights bill. He therefore had a significant impact on the lives of African Americans by bringing the problems that they faced to people's attention and persuading the government to do something about it.

   b) Malcolm X encouraged African Americans to take pride in their African heritage. His preaching helped to raise African-American confidence and self-esteem.

   c) Stokely Carmichael popularised the idea of 'Black Power', arguing that racism and inequality could only be tackled by strengthening black communities and making them more independent of white society. These ideas were embraced by the Black Panther Party, who worked to improve the lives of African Americans by protecting them from violence and carrying out education and healthcare programmes.

Page 51 — The Civil Rights Acts of 1964 and 1968

Knowledge and Understanding

1   Johnson succeeded because he was a skilful negotiator, and was able to use the wave of emotion that followed Kennedy's assassination to gain support for the bill.

2   • It banned discrimination in public facilities like hotels, restaurants, theatres and parks.

    • It encouraged the desegregation of public schools and universities.

    • It promoted equal access to jobs and banned workplace discrimination.

    • It made rules against discrimination in voter registration stronger.

3   The 1968 Civil Rights Act was introduced to stop racial discrimination in housing. Before 1968, African Americans were often prevented from buying or renting homes in certain areas, forcing them to live in overcrowded and poorly built neighbourhoods. However, the act made it illegal to refuse to sell or rent a house to someone because of their race, colour, religion or nationality.

4   The powers of the authorities to enforce the act were limited and people continued to discriminate against African Americans in housing in ways that were less obvious and harder to prove. For example, many estate agents continued to steer African Americans away from white neighbourhoods. This meant that the act failed to encourage integration.

Interpretation

1   You can answer either way, as long as you explain your answers. For example:

   a) This is convincing because America had lacked a national Civil Rights law until the 1964 Civil Rights Act was passed. From 1964, the federal government had the power to protect minorities from discrimination in every state.

   b) This is only partially convincing because Congress did pass legislation to prevent discrimination in the US Army in the 1940s. For example, it passed a law making segregation in the US Army illegal in 1948. However, this had a limited impact because it didn't affect all African Americans, only those in the Army.

2   The interpretation might give a positive view of the 1964 Civil Rights Act because its authors were heavily involved in the act becoming law. Filvaroff was a government official who helped to draft the act, and Wolfinger was an assistant to one of the senators who helped to get it passed by Congress. Their personal involvement in the act makes them more likely to present it positively.

Page 53 — The 'Great Society'

Knowledge and Understanding

1   • It increased the minimum wage from $1 an hour to $1.25 for over 27 million workers.

    • Approximately 4.4 million people received new or increased social security benefits.

    • The Manpower and Training Act of 1962 gave unemployed people the opportunity to retrain.

2   The 'New Frontier' programme didn't go as far as Kennedy wanted because Congress opposed some of his plans to introduce affordable healthcare and investment in education.

3   • Economic Opportunity Act (1964) — This introduced a Job Corps to give training to young people and help them to find jobs. It also gave grants for adult education and provided assistance to needy children.

    • Elementary and Secondary Education Act (1965) — This gave funds to schools with poorer children.

    • Higher Education Act (1965) — This gave student loans to people who struggled to afford university.

    • Social Security Act (1965) — This introduced Medicare to provide basic healthcare to people over 65 years old, and Medicaid to provide basic healthcare to those who were too poor to afford it.

Interpretation

1   Interpretation 1 gives a more positive view of the 'Great Society', as Levitan says that it tried to 'ensure the wellbeing of all citizens' and to make society more equal. Interpretation 2 gives a more negative view, as Nixon says that the services provided by the 'Great Society' discouraged 'self-reliance' by making people dependent on help from the government.

2   Here are some points your answer may include:

    • The authors might have different views because of their different political beliefs. Levitan helped the Democratic Party to create policies for Kennedy's 'New Frontier' programme, so is likely to support Johnson's 'Great Society' programme too. However, Nixon was a Republican who had different views on how to tackle poverty, making him more likely to criticise the Democratic Party's approach.

    • The authors might have different views because they were writing for different purposes. Levitan was writing an article for a journal, so is likely to analyse the impact of the 'Great Society' in a more impartial way. However, Nixon was writing his memoirs, making him more likely to criticise Johnson's policies in an attempt to justify the changes that he made after he was elected.

Answers

Page 55 — Women's Rights
Knowledge and Understanding
1 a) It investigated inequality between men and women at work and in America's taxation and legal systems, before publishing a report in October 1963. The report suggested that discrimination against women was a serious problem and criticised gender inequality in America.
   b) It made it illegal for women to be paid less than men for the same job.
   c) It banned discrimination in employment on the basis of sex.
2 NOW was the National Organisation for Women. It was founded by activists who were frustrated with the EEOC's failure to enforce equality at work in order to campaign for women's legal, educational and professional equality.
3 • Gender equality should be written into the Constitution.
   • Women should have access to equal employment rights and job opportunities.
   • Women should be allowed to take paid maternity leave.
   • Women should have access to child care.
   • Women should have the right to have an abortion.
4 • They petitioned the EEOC and demonstrated at EEOC offices.
   • They disrupted Senate hearings.
   • They launched legal challenges to sex discrimination.
   • They organised marches.
   • They boycotted companies that discriminated against women.

Thinking Historically
1 a) Women were limited to certain roles because of gender stereotypes. They were expected to be housewives and mothers, which made it difficult for women to pursue a career. In the 1960s, women only made up around 33-43% of the workforce.
   b) Women who did work were restricted to certain jobs, such as cleaning, nursing and teaching. They didn't receive equal pay, earning on average 40% less than men.
   c) The laws that were meant to tackle discrimination in the workplace, such as the 1963 Equal Pay Act and the 1964 Civil Rights Act, were not enforced properly. The EEOC focused on racial discrimination and failed to take gender discrimination seriously. This meant that employers were able to get around the laws, for example by giving different job titles to men and women who were doing the same job.

Page 57 — Women's Rights
Knowledge and Understanding
1 a) The Equal Pay Act had banned gender discrimination in pay for a lot of jobs, but the Educational Amendments Act extended it to executive, administrative and professional jobs.
   b) The Civil Rights Act banned gender discrimination at work, not in public education. The Educational Amendments Act forced public educational establishments to provide equal facilities and opportunities for both sexes.
2 The Hyde Amendment was a law passed by Congress in 1976 that stopped Medicaid from funding abortions. It was passed in response to pressure from religious groups.
3 The ERA was the Equal Rights Amendment, a constitutional amendment to guarantee equal rights for women. Some women opposed it because they wanted a return to traditional femininity. This meant that they didn't believe in equality between men and women, and wanted women to be protected and provided for in their role as wives and mothers.

4 The ERA had to be ratified by 38 of America's 50 states for it to become law. However, Phyllis Schlafly's 'STOP ERA' campaign slowed down the ratification process, and some states that had already ratified the amendment withdrew their support. In the end, the ERA was only ratified by 35 states, so it didn't become law.

Thinking Historically
1 a) The Supreme Court ruled that it was discrimination under the 14th Amendment for men to take priority if two people claimed to be equally entitled to a relative's inheritance.
   b) This was the first time that the 14th Amendment, which guarantees equal protection under the law to all citizens, had been used to protect women's rights.
   c) The Supreme Court ruled that state laws banning abortion were unconstitutional.
   d) It meant that women now had the right to choose whether or not they wanted an abortion. This gave women more power over their own bodies.
2 Here are some points your answer may include:
   • Point — Some political campaigns helped to maintain gender inequality, rather than reducing it.
   • Evidence — Phyllis Schlafly staged rallies to pressure states into rejecting the ERA as part of the 'STOP ERA' campaign. Some states withdrew their support for the ERA as a result, and it was never ratified.
   • Why evidence supports point? — The failure to ratify the ERA was a serious blow to women's rights activists, because it meant that equal rights for women still weren't guaranteed by the Constitution. Schlafly's 'STOP ERA' campaign limited women's progress in the fight for equality.
   • Point — Rulings by the Supreme Court meant that women's rights were protected by the law.
   • Evidence — In 1971, the Supreme Court ruled in the case Reed v Reed that laws discriminating against women were unconstitutional. It went on to issue rulings against gender discrimination in employment later in 1971 and in 1973.
   • Why evidence supports point? — These rulings gave legal protection to women in a way that hadn't been done before, and showed that the Supreme Court was willing to use the 14th Amendment to protect women's rights. The Supreme Court's rulings were therefore important in reducing gender inequality.
   • Point — The progress made by some legal rulings was undone by the government.
   • Evidence — In 1973, the Supreme Court ruled in the case Roe v Wade that state laws banning abortion were unconstitutional. However, the Hyde Amendment was passed three years later, making abortion too expensive for poorer women.
   • Why evidence supports point? — Roe v Wade gave women power over their own bodies, but the Hyde Amendment took it away again from women who couldn't afford an abortion. This suggests that legal rulings weren't always enough to reduce inequality.

Page 63 — Exam-Style Questions
1 This question is level marked. How to grade your answer:

Level 1 1-2 marks	The answer shows appropriate knowledge of the period by identifying at least one relevant difficulty.
Level 2 3-4 marks	The answer shows appropriate knowledge and understanding of the period by identifying two relevant difficulties and explaining each one.

Answers

Here are some points your answer may include:

- One difficulty that African Americans faced was being forced to live as second-class citizens due to segregation. Jim Crow Laws meant that workplaces, schools and a wide range of other public facilities were all segregated. In theory, these facilities were meant to be 'separate but equal'. In reality, public facilities for African Americans were a lot worse than the ones available to white people.

- Jim Crow Laws meant that it was difficult for African Americans in the South to get a good education. Schools for African-American pupils received far less money than schools for white pupils, because white-controlled local governments were in charge of allocating funding. This often meant that African-American schools were overcrowded, had poor-quality buildings and lacked resources.

- Another difficulty that African Americans faced due to Jim Crow Laws was a lack of employment opportunities. The laws barred African Americans from skilled jobs in industry and from most professional and office jobs, so most African Americans worked as farm labourers.

2   This question is level marked. How to grade your answer:

Level 1 1-2 marks	The answer describes one or more changes, but doesn't explain them. Some knowledge and understanding of the period is shown.
Level 2 3-4 marks	The answer describes some valid changes and explains one of them in more detail. Appropriate knowledge and understanding of the period is shown.
Level 3 5-6 marks	The answer explains two or more changes in detail. A good level of knowledge and understanding of the period is used to support the explanations.
Level 4 7-8 marks	The answer explains more complex patterns of change. Excellent knowledge and understanding of the period is used to support the explanations.

Here are some points your answer may include:

- The 1964 Civil Rights Act gave African Americans in the South equal access to public facilities. Segregation had forced them to use separate facilities to white people since the introduction of Jim Crow Laws in the late 19th century. However, the act forced the federal government to take action against these state laws and protect African Americans from discrimination.

- The 1964 Civil Rights Act allowed African Americans to become more involved in politics. Previously, the 15th Amendment hadn't been enforced in the South, and most African Americans were prevented from voting by racist laws. However, the act strengthened rules against discrimination in voter registration. All of the obstacles that prevented African Americans from voting were only officially removed by the Voting Rights Act in 1965, but the Civil Rights Act was still an important step.

- It became easier for African Americans in the South to receive a good education as a result of the 1964 Civil Rights Act. The act encouraged the desegregation of public schools and universities, many of which remained segregated in the South due to opposition to the 1954 Brown v Board of Education ruling. This meant that many African Americans were still attending separate schools that received far less funding than white schools. However, the act allowed them to go to the same schools as white students, and to receive a better education as a result.

- After the 1964 Civil Rights Act, African Americans gained more employment opportunities. The act promoted equal access to job opportunities, and banned discrimination in the workplace. This led to the introduction of 'affirmative action', which meant that businesses and government agencies actively tried to increase the number of people from under-represented groups (including African Americans) that they employed.

- The 1968 Civil Rights Act gave some African Americans the right to live wherever they wanted. The act made it illegal to refuse to sell or rent a house to someone due to their race. This meant that some African Americans were no longer forced to live in overcrowded and poorly built neighbourhoods away from white communities. However, the government had limited powers to enforce the act, and people continued to discriminate against African Americans in less obvious ways. For example, estate agents often steered African American clients away from white neighbourhoods.

- Many African Americans in the North experienced minimal change as a result of the Civil Rights Acts. They thought that the acts did little to tackle the discrimination that they faced, and made little difference to their lives. The ineffectiveness of the acts meant that some northern African Americans started to turn to more aggressive protest methods. There were over 750 inner-city riots involving African Americans between 1964 and 1972.

3   This question is level marked. How to grade your answer:

Level 1 1-3 marks	The answer shows limited knowledge and understanding of the period. It explains one or both bullet points in a general way.
Level 2 4-6 marks	The answer shows some appropriate knowledge and understanding of the period. It gives a simple analysis of one or both bullet points, using knowledge of the period to justify its points.
Level 3 7-9 marks	The answer shows a good level of appropriate knowledge and understanding of the period. It analyses both bullet points in more detail, using knowledge of the period to justify its points.
Level 4 10-12 marks	The answer shows detailed and precise knowledge and understanding of the period. It analyses both bullet points in detail, using knowledge of the period to justify its points. It makes connections between the bullet points and comes to a clear conclusion about which one was more important.

Here are some points your answer may include:

- America's post-war prosperity led to important social changes, as many Americans became 'middle class'. This is because wages and employment levels increased after the war and people could afford a much higher standard of living. This was a welcome change from the poverty and hardship that a lot of Americans had experienced during the Depression.

- America experienced a baby boom after the Second World War, which was partly a consequence of post-war prosperity. As more people earned enough income to support a family, the birth rate increased dramatically and the population rose by over 12 million between 1945 and 1950.

Answers

- Another social change that America experienced due to post-war prosperity was the development of the suburbs. The demand for housing grew as people gained enough income to start a family, causing a house-building boom. Many of these houses were built outside cities in the suburbs, attracting people from rural and urban areas. The growth of these suburbs led to other social changes, like the construction of suburban shopping malls, which gave people a place to shop and socialise.

- Although post-war prosperity improved living standards for many Americans, it also led to increasing inequality. Outside 'suburbia', 25% of Americans still lived in poverty. African Americans in inner-city neighbourhoods and people in rural areas like Appalachia were especially badly affected. This meant that living comfortably in the suburbs wasn't an option for everyone in America.

- America's post-war prosperity led to important cultural changes. For example, consumerism became a major features of Americans' lives, as more and more people had enough money to buy luxury goods like cars, televisions and record players. However, social changes such as the development of shopping malls also played a role in creating this culture of consumerism, as they also encouraged people to buy luxury goods.

- America's prosperity made popular culture more accessible in the post-war period. An increase in prosperity meant that people had an average of five times more money to spend on things like cinema, music and fashion in 1955 than they did in 1940. Many people could also afford a television, with around 50 million households owning one by 1960.

- The creation of a separate 'teenage' culture was another important cultural change in post-war America. The growing prosperity of some American families meant that young people had more money than ever before, which allowed them to become more involved in popular culture. Teenagers responded by developing their own culture based on the ideas of freedom and defiance. Older people disapproved of some aspects of this culture, such as rock and roll music, which led to the creation of a generation gap.

- The social changes that took place as a consequence of America's post-war prosperity were more important than the cultural changes. This is because social changes sometimes prompted cultural changes. For example, a culture of consumerism might not have developed when it did without social changes like the development of shopping malls.

Index